BRIGHT IDEAS

Inspirations for GEOGRAPHY

Published by Scholastic
Publications Ltd,
Villiers House,
Clarendon Avenue,
Leamington Spa,
Warwickshire CV32 5PR

© 1993 Heather Norris Nicholson

Written by Heather Norris
Nicholson
Edited by Felicity Kendall
Sub-edited by Jane Wright
Designed by Anna Oliwa
Series designed by Juanita
Puddifoot
Illustrated by David Williams
Cover design by Micky Pledge
Cover artwork by Caroline Porter

Designed using Aldus Pagemaker
Processed by Studio Photoset,
Leicester
Artwork by Steve Williams &
Associates, Leicester
Printed in Great Britain by
Ebenezer Baylis & Son, Worcester

**British Library Cataloguing in
Publication Data**
A catalogue record for this book is
available from the British Library.

ISBN 0-590-53046-1

CONTENTS

INTRODUCTION

Geography

Who are we? Where are we? Where do we come from? Children's discoveries about themselves, their society and their surroundings are part of their personal development. These concerns are also the essence of primary geography and justify its place in the primary curriculum.

Once, geography – or earth writing in its most literal sense – was a means to describe and label uncharted territory. Much later, rote-learning of a medley of names, facts and other geographical bric-a-brac became a means to instil an awareness of colonial pride and purpose. Ever-responsive to the needs of a changing world, geography now brings into focus critical concerns about the state of society, the planet and life on earth.

Every day other people, places and predicaments are brought to our attention through advertisements, television and other media. Often this information is far from complete and gives a false impression. There needs to be a place in the primary curriculum where the children can sort out fact from fantasy. There also should be a place where children can address issues that affect them directly, such as environmental quality and social well-being.

This book urges teachers to respond to the challenge and importance of geography in children's development. Its purpose is to kindle enthusiasm, encourage purposeful and imaginative teaching, and foster critical awareness through geographical understanding. This writing stems from a personal commitment to geography as a means to perceive and make sense of a fascinating, yet at times confusing and inherently contradictory world. It should be seen as nothing more than a springboard from which teachers, according to their experience, interests and circumstances, may be able to explore other geographical possibilities though a combination of practical suggestions, issue-raising and reflection.

BACKGROUND

How to use this book

This book is divided into three sections which deal with different aspects of geographical teaching and learning. The first section explores how human, physical and environmental geography may be developed through varied activities in and beyond the classroom. The second section focuses on different approaches to primary geography, such as the use of stories, photography and information technology in planned activities. The third section considers links with other subject areas and cross-curricular elements, strategies for planning and aspects of assessment. Since treating themes, ways of working and scales of enquiry separately may seem to impose artificial boundaries, it is important that teachers dip into different chapters, and make their connections between themes, places and methods as appropriate.

The introduction to each chapter indicates the key issues to consider. In most chapters this is followed by practical teaching ideas and activities.

Guidelines accompany the practical activities and suggest their suitability for different ages or abilities. However, teachers must decide what seems appropriate for particular children's needs and the amount of time deemed necessary for adequate study of a topic. Sometimes further activities are indicated, so that teachers may plan for differentiation and progression. How each activity or group of similar activities matches statutory requirements is indicated in the Attainment Target Chart at the end of the book. Links with other subject areas are common to many activities and explored in Chapters 11 and 12. Finally, there is a useful chapter of resources and a set of photocopiable pages including five blank outline maps for general use and specific sheets which relate directly to particular activities and will save time in the busy classroom.

CHAPTER 1

Being at school

Young children spend a considerable amount of their waking moments at school. It represents a significant proportion of their own lives and is one of the closest experiences they share with other children. Going to school for the very first time marks a significant stage in life: its subsequent routines, expectations and encounters may offer some children stability, excitement and opportunities lacking elsewhere in their lives.

School often involves meeting larger numbers of other children than ever before; it brings new levels of independence and personal responsibility and requires learning to be part of a wider whole. More complex and extensive relationships with other people, places and objects require significant changes in behaviour, attitude, knowledge and understanding. These socialisation processes are integral to being at school and offer an excellent basis for fostering the development of young children's geographical awareness.

BACKGROUND

Making geographical discoveries

For many children, exploring the world they live in starts long before coming to school, providing foundations for later spatial awareness and geographical understanding. Recognition of surroundings, distinctive places, spaces, people and things may be implicit in their drawings, play, conversation and behaviour. Stories, other people talking, personal experiences, television and pictures may have introduced them already to geographical words, ideas and concerns about the world around them. Finding a way to value, encourage and extend this prior learning is as important as the need to build on more limited experience.

Many aspects of young children's everyday activities and experiences may have a geographical dimension. The buildings they live in or visit comprise interconnected spaces with distinctive character and are usually associated with particular activities. Visits to shops, the local clinic or park and relatives involve routes, passing things, changing directions, distance and time, views, vantage points, surfaces, boundaries, places and processes, which pave the way for later understanding.

Observations from this knee-high view of the world introduce notions of people, place, preference and predicaments which strengthen subsequent fieldwork skills and geographical understanding. Indeed, these discoveries about the world around them may sometimes provide a sounder base for geographical enquiry, than the experiences of the well-travelled child for whom journeys have ceased to be an adventure.

Very young children make geographical discoveries through indirect encounters and experiences. Their imaginative games, the imitative portrayal of observed actions and behaviour, as well

Christmas Work

Class 4 - Sketching Nature Trail

OUR TOWN

Class 4's Rabb.

as their use or improvisation of toys, often reflect children's spatial awareness and sense of surroundings. Responses to picture books, storytelling, nursery rhymes and songs may indicate recognition of place and action, and practice of geographical vocabulary and patterns of association. This early abstract awareness obviously varies, but its encouragement is an important foundation for later geographical understanding.

Geography has much appeal and relevance for young children. As they explore, they develop motor, communication and social skills which strengthen investigations in and beyond the classroom and support continuing encounters through story, music, art and other cross-curricular activities. Although recognisable in curriculum planning as early geographical experiences, these activities are more integrated in the children's minds.

Informal approaches complement these activities and encourage children's responses, curiosity and enjoyment of the world around them. Painting, drawing, sand play and the use of construction materials, programmable toys, jigsaws, inflatable globes, play-mats and picture-matching sets are significant in fostering the beginnings of school geography.

The geography of school

As a microcosm of the wider world, the school environment, community and organisation provide an excellent forum for early geography. As children become part of that functioning system of people and places, they learn to find their way, use and organise spaces, and join in with patterns of daily movement and activity which are dependent upon pre-determined procedures. As familiarity grows, children gain awareness about *where* people, places and things are and *how* they interrelate. *What* happens *where*, *who* does *what*, *when* and *where* certain activities occur, *how* and *why* things are organised are central to children's school experiences.

Geographical understanding derives from learning to appreciate different people's contributions to school life. It requires becoming responsible towards people and places and informs children's preferences about what to do and where to play. As their geographical skills and perceptions develop, they learn to recognise what is distinctive about where they live and go to school, how places change over time, and how different activities and peoples are found in different settings.

The school buildings, grounds and community are an accessible and safe

Within the illustration:

CLASSROOM

HALL

CORRIDOR

CLASSROOM

R. JONES P.N.I.N.W.
ST. JAMES SCHOOL

ST. JAMES GARDEN

GRASS

FOOTPATH

PEDESTRIAN

My School

My school is very big and has lots of rooms.
There are class rooms and a dining room and a room where we play games.
There are lots of trees and

A Plan of my school

Hall

4a

4b

2a

3a 3b

Playground

environment for geographical enquiry. Surveys, data gathering and practical observation over time are possible in this doorstep learning environment, where children can develop investigative skills with minimal practical difficulties. Any appraisal of the school site's potential for geography should look closely at the buildings.

Design and decoration may offer clues to the school's connections with the wider world and provide starting points for geographical enquiry. Maps, aerial or satellite photographs and pictures at child height, furnishings, fabric, music and instruments, food, artefacts, stories, dressing-up clothes, toys and even potted plants all in different but complementary ways raise awareness, stimulate curiosity and create an exciting learning environment for geography.

Geography and the school community

A school's members and visitors are an invaluable teaching resource. Their daily work offers a wealth of geographical data which, time and willingness permitting, pupils could gather, analyse, record, map and interpret in different ways. Work of this kind raises awareness of the complexity underlying the life, care and running of their school. People in school may be able to offer other geographical information too, about journeys, families, friends, living elsewhere, or holidays in different places. Unexpected connections with other localities and communities emerge from surveys and questionnaires. Mapping activities reveal patterns of interdependence, mobility and communication which reflect geographical processes at different scales.

Any class of children is full

of geographical possibilities! Details of where they live, where other family members live or their home-life and holidays or visits demonstrate some of the variety of experiences to explore. Class photographs, taken periodically from the first day at school, offer reminders about growth and seasonal change. Changing class composition invites investigation into where, why and how often people move. Maps, atlases and reference materials can be used to locate and find out more about places of origin or new destinations.

The children can use each other as a geographical resource by considering how people keep or lose contact with each other, and the challenges of being in a new place and trying to look at the familiar through unfamiliar eyes. Developing more informed understanding about themselves, other people and their surroundings is central to much of early school geography. This aim underlies many of the following activities which explore aspects of going to and being at school.

ACTIVITIES

1. Model classroom

Objective
This activity has several stages: the children consider how a box might represent their classroom setting and then discover how a two-dimensional plan might be developed from a three-dimensional model using their own observations.

Age range
Five and over.

Group size
Whole class and small groups work together to produce one box-model. Individual box-models of the classroom (or variations which include children modelling their bedroom or an imaginary room, perhaps from a story) would take longer and would have different learning goals and purpose.

What you need
A large cardboard box to represent the classroom with extra boxes and cardboard for ceiling and adjacent spaces, several large sheets of plain paper, art materials, scissors, paste, tape.

What to do
Ask the children to imagine that the cardboard box is their classroom. Discuss with them what they might do to give it identity. As a class, brainstorm and gather words to describe the classroom. List the suggestions either on the board or on a large sheet of paper.

Ask the children to identify the position of walls, doors, windows and the carpeted area within the box. Discuss with them how to mark these features and how to add furnishings and/or labels.

Get the children to work in small groups or individually to make features of the model classroom. They could find pictures, or draw objects, furniture and features on pre-cut paper, which will fit into the box. They will need to write labels and assemble the model with furnishings and decorations. Ceilings may be added with light fittings, skylights and so on. Discuss with the children how they might put themselves and you into the model at an appropriate scale, for instance, using models, pictures or toy figures.

Further activities
Place paper underneath the box-model and draw an outline to give a simple plan. Remove the box and ask the children to identify where parts of the model now approximate to the plan. Get them to practise positioning labels and features from the model to the plan to establish relationships. You can introduce simple letter or number coordinates by using squared paper.

Transfer the outline plan from a horizontal to a wall surface allowing time for this new perspective to be grasped. Using labels to mark

features or cut-out figures of the children, let them practise matching these, to consolidate the shift from concrete to abstract form.

Add other details to the vertical plan. Involve the children in finding practical ways to represent features on the plan now that it is fixed vertically. Problem-solving means finding how to mark positions of features in symbolic form using writing, letters, colour or pictures.

Once the relationship between box, plan and place is established, other options are possible. You can ask the children to model adjacent spaces to the classroom, and extend the outline plan to show other people and activities associated with these surrounding areas. Space, time, coordination and a lot of boxes are required for more ambitious models: a playground or school hall version constructed in one day by a whole year group makes for exciting collaborative work, particularly if timed to coincide with a visit from a feeder first school!

Extending the model clearly requires colleagues' cooperation in enabling children to identify and survey different parts of the school beyond their own classroom.

2. A school who's who

Objective

To talk with people who work in different areas of the school. This activity gives value to other people's contributions to school life and locates each child within a wider physical context and school community.

Age range

All ages.

Group size

Whole class, although interviews might be more suited to small groups (paired-work with mixed age-groups could assist interview techniques).

What you need

Large and small sheets of paper, pencils, clipboards, cassette recorders for practice interviews, word processor, plan of school, local map, display and presentation materials.

What to do

Discuss with the children the different kinds of work people do within the school. Identify the areas of the school that they work in. Devise appropriate questions for interviews. Questions might include: 'Where do you work in the school?', 'What kinds of work do you do?'and 'What do you like least/most about your work?' In pairs children should practise effective interview techniques through role play.

Questionnaires and surveys on other aspects of people's lives might provide other data which could be mapped, sorted and interpreted, depending upon the focus of the investigation. Some questionnaires could be devised and printed out from a word processor, if available.

Further activities

Recollections of past times or specific events offer clues into how the school site and community have changed. Photographs and artefacts might be gathered as part of this foray into the school's past.

Questions on place of birth and where members of the school have lived provide data on mobility, which may be mapped and compared with information from another school or the wider local area.

cleaner   caretaker   head teacher   class teacher   student teacher

These shared stories and personal biographies all promote a sense of identity and belonging to a school community. Out of such geographical enquiries might come cross-curricular initiatives such as a book on the individual and collective memories of being at school, or a tea towel representing everyone (ideal for fund-raising).

3. Passing places

Objective
To develop a sense of routes and journeys using an earlier walk close to the school (see also Chapter 4).

Age range
Five and over.

Group size
Small groups or whole class with helpers.

What you need
Large sheets of paper, felt pens, adhesive, camera, photographs taken on the walk.

What to do
Take the children on a walk in the immediate vicinity of the school. Take photographs of distinctive features of the surroundings as you progress. Tell the children to try to remember all that they experience on the walk for a discussion later on.

Later on, after the photographs have been developed, ask the children about what they saw, heard, touched, felt and encountered above, below and around them on the walk. Brainstorm the things passed and pictures taken, before introducing and identifying the photographs. Reconstruct the journey by inviting the children to close their eyes and imagine the walk.

Arrange the photographs in sequence on a flat surface, discussing the order with the children and offering clues as required.

Divide the journey into stages between photo-stops. Use large sheets of paper and ask the children in turn to draw each section, marking in the route, and drawing things passed. Ask them to consider how to show bends and turnings along the route, distance between photo-stops, ups and downs or other features of the route. Add the photographs and devise labels. Add a title and then mount the map at children's level.

Further activities
Display on an adjoining surface any items collected or rubbings made during the walk and link them by thread to the appropriate place along the route.

Add children's writing about 'What I remember or liked most or least ...'.
• Develop thematic walks where street furniture, patterns, building features, sounds and textures could be sequenced (see Chapter 7, page 101 'Theme walks'). Devise a trail using pictures of features as clues for another class or visitors to follow.
• Devise a route to or around the school for someone who cannot see. What clues could they use? A walk around school, with pairs being blindfolded in turn, usually helps children to appreciate the value of non-visual clues.

4. Inside out

Objective
To focus attention on the school environment by looking for visual clues about use and utilities. This activity could also use other buildings in the immediate locality.

Age range
Any age.

Group size
Whole class or small groups.

What you need
Drawing materials, pencil, clipboard or notebook, camera or other recording materials for utilities survey, outline plan of the school, large-scale local map or enlarged street plan, reference books.

What to do
Allocate children to specific sections of the school. Ask them to look for observable clues which identify what goes on inside – pipes, windows, entrances, signs, chimney or air vents, aerials, wires, drain covers, fans and so on.

Get the children to classify the utilities according to their function and consider the routes of water, electricity, gas, drains, chimney, central heating and so on within a building. These should be plotted on an outline plan of the school.

Using a large-scale map or their own drawings, the children can trace school or house utilities to the main network in the local street or area. Discuss with them the impact of utilities which are out of service and the kinds of work necessary to maintain the system.

Ask the children to compare the school utilities with those

for other buildings in the area or in a contrasting place. Comparisons with different building styles in different parts of the world might include: discussion of extreme temperatures, earth movements, flood protection, health hazards and contrasting lifestyles.

Further activities
Does a building have wrinkles? Look for clues which suggest processes of change, such as extensions, adaptations, different entrances and new car parks. Look for changes of building materials, style, decoration, lettering or special features. Record these in sketch or note form. Older features may be suitable for wax rubbings, prints, plaster casts or tin-foil relief work.

Discuss the information gathered and the possible reasons for the observed differences and changes through time. Compare this with pictures of older buildings in the local area or a contrasting place. Use evidence as clues to lifestyles

in the past. If changes to buildings are within living memory, try to find someone who can talk about the site as it used to be.

5. Cosy corners

Objective
To raise environmental awareness and explore the relationship between physical character and use of site.

Age range
Seven to eight.

Group size
Whole class and individuals, depending on the parts of the activity.

What you need
Drawing and recording materials, clipboard, compass, photocopiable page 185; outline plans of the school.

Extension activities might use practical materials and require contact with specialist planners, architects or landscape designers.

What to do
Allocate children to different parts of the school site. Using photocopiable page 185, ask them to identify and record different aspects of the school grounds (windy/sheltered, warm/cool, sunny/shady). Encourage them to relate their findings to weather, seasonal change, physical setting and compass direction.

Next, ask the children to record areas of the site which are busy, noisy, quiet, peaceful and so on, and to identify attractive/unattractive areas and features. Remind them to consider front and back views of the school, position of the kitchen, dustbins, the incinerator, and so on.

Finally, bring the children together to compare such findings and discuss their preferences and reasons and potential for change. Could seats, paths, litter bins be put in other places? Could plants and bushes make any area more attractive? Could the playground be made into a safer or more interesting place? Are there any eyesores? Could they be disguised or removed?

Further activities
Such ideas could become a basis for practical environmental improvement of the school site (see Chapter 7) or lead on to creative design work and writing about an ideal school setting.

6. Traffic jams

Objective
To consider patterns of movement within the school.

Age range
Eight and over.

Group size
Whole class, although survey work is best done in pairs.

What you need
An outline school plan, acetate overlays, pens, writing materials, graph paper.

What to do
Ask the children to identify when the school is quiet and when it is busy. Consider if some parts of the school are used more than others. Discuss with them where and when different people move around school.

Ask them to list reasons for movement and numbers or groups of people involved. Can they identify how movement in the school is organised at busy times and suggest why rules might help when large numbers of people are involved?

In small groups or pairs, get the children to devise a traffic code to assist movement of people around the school. They could show movement of people and goods around the school using flow lines on an outline plan or overlays.

Further activities
• Devise a one-way system for the school site and investigate its impact on the length of journeys and congestion.
• Survey car parking provision and congestion. Devise a route around the car park.
• Investigate how congestion at school entrances might be reduced during busy periods.
• Design a way-marking system for the school site and consider the position of signs, use of colour and lettering. Try out the system and survey the response of another class or visitors in the school.

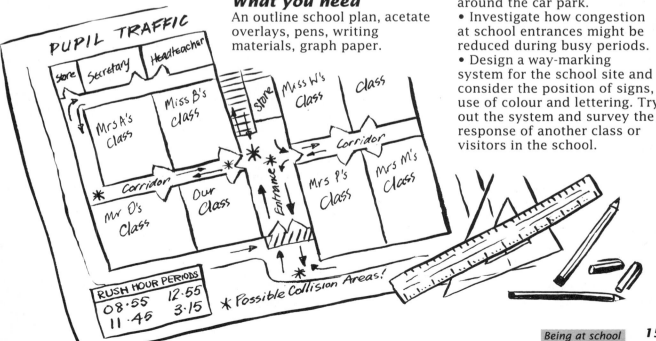

7. Postal survey

Objective
To identify communication links between individuals, the school and other localities.

Age range
Seven and over.

Group size
Individuals.

What you need
Outline maps of Britain, Europe and the world (see photocopiable pages 180–184), wall maps or atlases, writing materials, photocopiable page 186, postage stamps, reference materials, paper.

What to do
Discuss with the children the different types of post which may be delivered at home and school. Using photocopiable page 186, conduct a class or individual survey on where post has come from over a five-day period (minimum) at home or school. Ask the children to plot the origins on outline maps using an atlas to check locations.

Finally, the children could trace the journey of the post (including the different types of transport used) along various stages of route. Suggest they could also survey where post has been sent to from home or school over the same time period. In the survey, encourage the children to think about the length of journey both in terms of distance travelled and time taken.

Further activities
• Activities such as writing letters, visiting post offices (and sorting offices) or dispatch points, inviting a postal worker to visit the school and so on, could expand this work on postal links between people and places.
• A collection of used postage stamps may also provide an interesting source of local/distant contacts (and when finished with, can be sent to charities). Children may consider details about the origin, currency and design of the stamps and plot on a map their community's postal links with elsewhere.
• The children could go on to consider any other different connections between home, school and the wider area.

Reflections

Activities in this chapter explore geographical aspects of being at school. Some activities encourage awareness and understanding of how the school and school community work and how school life connects with the world beyond. Other activities reveal how each individual helps to shape patterns of continuity and change. All may help young children to gain a sense of identity and belonging, which contributes to their positive involvement in and beyond school.

Use of the school must be planned carefully so that there is minimal disruption and children's interest is sustained. School-based enquiry must build on earlier skills and prior learning. There must be progressive and systematic development of fieldwork and classroom skills in parallel to children's overall development. The geography of being at school provides an essential foundation for geographical teaching and learning across the entire primary phase and thus plays a critical point in whole school planning.

Comparisons with other schools may be firmly rooted in an appreciation of personal experiences and school identity. Chapter 2 suggests ways to compare school life elsewhere using electronic mail, video or exchanges of children's work. School links are equally valid at a local level and offer the possibility of children visiting each other where practical difficulties of movement between sites are surmountable.

The benefits of meeting other pupils and exchanging ideas about locality, community, lifestyle and interests undeniably enrich the geography curriculum. Sharing experiences of homes, travel and school, concerns with wider environmental issues through presentations, chaired discussion, displays, role plays and the effectiveness of board games and trails not only bring variety into teaching and learning, but foster important social, study and communication skills.

CHAPTER 2

Fieldwork

Although imaginative teaching takes children's thinking on journeys of considerable distance, fieldwork remains at the heart of geography. First-hand encounters with other places, people's relationship with their surroundings and direct observation of processes, must underpin geographical education.

Work beyond the classroom, even in the school grounds or immediate vicinity of the school, provides a vital bridge to increasing children's understanding of the relevance of geography on a global scale.

This chapter explores how different fieldwork locations may help children to develop varied skills of research, analysis and interpretation. It identifies some of the curriculum potential and organisational implications for fieldwork in contrasting contexts. Planning for coherent fieldwork experiences across the primary phase is discussed in Chapter 13.

BACKGROUND

Fieldwork and geography

Effective learning is usually both memorable and enjoyable. Traditionally, fieldwork has often been the most remembered aspect of school geography. One reason may be its tendency to involve children and staff in making discoveries about their surroundings, and even about each other! A shared sense of purpose and relevance underlies meaningful fieldwork. Opportunities to investigate together may strengthen working relationships, motivate learning and foster both enthusiasm for and commitment to environmental understanding and awareness.

Fieldwork should link closely to the children's own interests, experiences and capabilities. Children should practise different learning skills and gain confidence and competence as they take part in original and first-hand research. Exploring familiar and new localities should be part of all children's geographical experience, and be clearly related to previous and subsequent learning activities.

During fieldwork activities, children work with their own unique set of findings. Their involvement not only builds on classroom understanding, but gives new meaning to the study of place and people's relationship with their surroundings. As children now construct ideas about the world from so many received images and fragmented impressions, building into the curriculum encounters with real places, people and processes is of fundamental importance. Indeed, when image precedes reality as a result of advertising, television or film, the fieldwork opportunities in geography become a critical part of planning for children's experience and development.

Fieldwork with meaning

Underlying all fieldwork should be a clear sense of investigation. First-hand research brings new awareness of familiar places and takes problem-solving into unfamiliar localities. Fieldwork should enable children to explore issues, test hypotheses or make personal responses using a range of techniques and sources of evidence. Clear notions of intended outcomes may influence the choice of subjective or objective ways of working. Different approaches will involve children in different types of information, skills and follow-up work.

Detailed fieldwork observation requires children to interpret environmental clues alongside other sources of written, numerical, visual or oral evidence.

Geographical observation need not be an end in itself. Gathered data becomes more exciting to collect and use when related to a particular problem or issue. Attempts to describe, locate and explain,

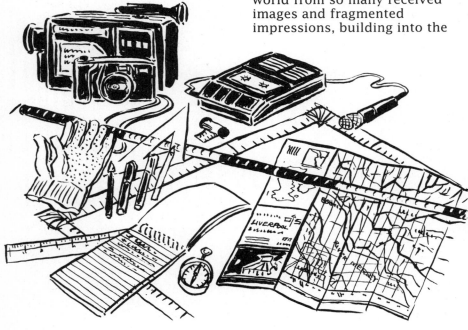

gain meaning through practice and application.

Young children's awareness about aspects of environmental quality, social well-being and aesthetic preference, often stem from a practical involvement in issues of local and personal interest. As children's concerns about global and environmental issues increase, fieldwork will offer some scope for responses and action which will balance abstract knowledge and understanding.

Fieldwork provides opportunities for more individual forms of self-expression and interpretation through art, drama, music or creative writing. Subjective responses based on careful observations are important as the children familiarise themselves with their environment. Finding different ways to present fieldwork may prompt closer links with other curricular areas, as children share their observations, analysis and interpretation through video, IT, role-play, the expressive arts and other activities.

Skills and techniques

Fieldwork skills include many generic study skills. Intellectual skills include the ability to observe, record, classify, analyse, interpret and apply information in an organised response to a hypothesis or problem. Social skills are involved as children make decisions, carry out intentions and share equipment, ideas and information. Communication skills include sharing data, expressing ideas, understanding viewpoints and generally being able to work effectively with other people.

Specific fieldwork skills include environmental detective work. Detailed observations may be recorded on maps, field sketches and tables, or in numerical and written form. Gathering data may be structured and require responses to pre-determined questions in a systematic manner or be more open-ended in form. Observations may require taking samples back to the classroom for later investigation. Some children rapidly become adept at using camcorders, cameras and cassette recorders. Specialised equipment may require children to practise specific techniques during fieldwork both in and out of the classroom.

Fieldwork and maps

Mapping skills are usually an important aspect of fieldwork. Children use maps to locate their fieldwork site before leaving the classroom, to identify specific areas for their own individual or shared investigation and to trace the journey to the fieldwork location. Maps may record information while on site or form part of the overall interpretation and presentation of findings. Mapwork involves orientating and handling maps of varying scales, and reading symbols and co-ordinates. Maps can be used to follow routes, compass directions or instructions.

Making simple sketch maps or plans or annotating a pre-drawn version involves making decisions about recording information by word, colour, symbol or picture. Using such skills on fieldwork will clearly depend upon the children's spatial awareness, experience and capabilities. Information technology may also be used to draw maps and plans of fieldwork sites (see Chapter 3 and Chapter 10).

Fieldwork and values

Acceptable attitudes and forms of behaviour are vital within fieldwork. Investigations either on or away from the school site require cooperation and responsibility. Fieldwork necessitates that children are responsive to the instructions and advice of teachers, adult helpers and those helping with their enquiries. Different

situations will require different types of thoughtful behaviour and action. Sensible attitudes towards equipment and the environment within which they are working are essential at all times.

Fieldwork brings children into closer contact with people who visit, work or live in contrasting environments. Learning to perceive and understand other people's interests, beliefs and views, even if not sharing them, underlies enquiry into many geographical themes. Understanding other viewpoints should not obscure critical awareness, but rather encourage sensitive and informed responses to aspects of environmental quality and community well-being.

Children's competence in offering opinions and seeing alternatives clearly grows with experience. Investigations may involve children in seeking assistance from outside agencies as part of their search for acceptable solutions and remedial action. Geographical enquiry should lead to constructive criticism, balanced interpretations and positive recommendations.

Consideration of privacy, personal perspectives and feelings is essential, especially where people's cooperation is necessary for surveys and filling in questionnaires. Understanding the meaning and purpose behind codes of conduct in both town and countryside should be part of the preparation for any fieldwork beyond the school grounds.

Types of fieldwork

The type of fieldwork will influence working methods, the nature of the data and its subsequent use. Some fieldwork focuses on gathering information about the environment to build up knowledge and understanding. Alternatively, some fieldwork may require collecting data as part of a problem-solving activity. This involves children in examining observable patterns and processes as they seek answers or alternative interpretations.

Some fieldwork may focus upon a specific issue – real or imagined – and involve children in gathering information, examining evidence from different perspectives and becoming involved in making decisions or taking action. Recognising these options opens up exciting fieldwork opportunities for both objective and subjective approaches to geographical teaching and learning.

Preparing for fieldwork

Fieldwork must be carefully integrated with classroom teaching. Teachers should decide where to place fieldwork within an overall programme of work and consider whether a visit at the start, towards the middle or at the end is most appropriate. Deciding whether the visit is to stimulate initial interest, build on prior knowledge or to conclude a unit of work will influence the timing of fieldwork, as might physical or seasonal conditions, and availability of transport and helpers.

Fieldwork should offer insights and experiences not available in the classroom. A chosen site should offer scope for differentiated tasks, suited to all children's learning capabilities. Chosen locations must be safe settings for varied forms of work, with suitable access and supervision, appropriate stopping points and places for both small group work and gathering all the children together. Few places are entirely hazard free, but careful problem-spotting in advance can help to anticipate difficulties which may arise.

Long journeys should be kept only for fieldwork opportunities and experiences unavailable closer to school.

Sometimes children can help to make decisions on aspects of the work programme or plan the route. A shared sense of purpose and awareness of how fieldwork relates to other activities, usually focuses attention and improves behaviour. It is helpful to give instructions and explanations beforehand, but on-site reminders are essential too. If data is to be recorded systematically, children should see prepared sheets in advance. They should know how to carry and use any equipment being taken out on fieldwork. Field sketching improves with practice, but prior attempts in school or the use of frames helps children to show objects in space.

Helpers can respond to children's questions and focus investigation more effectively if they know the teacher's intentions in advance. Pre-circulated background information and briefing notes alert them to teaching and learning possibilities and often deal with practical considerations more effectively than by holding a meeting. Letters about practical and financial implications of fieldwork need circulating as early as possible.

Fieldwork should concentrate on practical investigation and leave the bulk of classification, interpretation and additional fact-finding until everyone is back in the classroom. Inevitably, some analysis and sorting of ideas happen constantly, but later follow-up work allows for more extensive investigation and enables the children to make the most of their time on site.

This chapter divides fieldwork opportunities loosely into urban and rural areas, although there is some overlap. Many excellent locations are not included but those that are should indicate further possibilities. The activities suggested also permit comparative work in localities beyond the reach of a day visit and could generate materials suitable for exchanging with other schools. As many activities share similar practical considerations, there follows a general statement on fieldwork activities:

Objective
To develop specific fieldwork skills in different locations.

Age range
Any age (depending upon the focus of the activity).

Group size
Whole class working in small supervised groups.

What you need
Specific needs vary between activities, but most require: recording materials, cassette recorders, cameras, camcorder, outline plans, paper, rulers, pencils, pens, clip-boards, maps, atlases, measuring materials and bags for specimens.

Fieldwork in contrasting places
Similar fieldwork methods may be used in different environments, as indicated in italics at the top of each section. The suitability of each method depends on the children's age and experience and the teaching aims. For some fieldwork sites permission may need to be obtained before the visit. The suggestions in this chapter are supplemented by ideas on particular themes or topics from other chapters. Relevant links with other sections are indicated by cross-references in the text.

ACTIVITIES

Fieldwork in urban areas

Other ideas and activities for streetwork within the immediate vicinity of the school are suggested in Chapter 1. Where links to thematic aspects of human activity exist, readers should look at Chapter 6. Activities and ideas applicable to the study of people and places as part of the local area may link with material in Chapter 4. Further suggestions for urban-based fieldwork which develop children's understanding of physical and environmental geography are included in Chapters 5 and 7.

I Parks and gardens

Some of these suggestions may be suitable for private gardens, graveyards, woodlands, landscaped parks or school sites. Surveys of human activities are also applicable to fieldwork in small settlements in rural areas or in coastal locations.

Public open spaces offer traffic-free places where many urban fieldwork activities are possible. Parks and gardens combine opportunities for geographical enquiry into physical and environmental processes, and offer scope for investigating human activity in a designed and furnished landscape.

1. Recording on a site plan
Get small groups of children to count, plot, measure or record physical, social and aesthetic aspects of the area using art, writing and number work. Then ask them to note the details onto an enlarged site plan using letters, symbols, colour, shading or numbers to record and classify information.

2. Fieldsketching
Some children could annotate simple outline sketches or make their own fieldsketches of clearly defined areas, skylines and distinctive features or parts of the gardenscape.

3. Measuring heights and distances
A small group of children could plot features such as trees, buildings, bridges and benches on to an enlarged site plan and then estimate heights, measure horizontal distances and compare pathways with straight-line distances.

4. Where materials come from
Another group of children could record details of materials used in park ornaments, such as fountains, pools, terraces and sculpture and also origins of vegetation. Then they could try to map connections between locally occurring plant species or features and their places of origin using an atlas and an outline map.

5. Patterns of use
Ask the children to survey areas for evidence of shelter, shade, noise, pollution, types and levels of activity. Encourage them to relate patterns of use to age, gender,

activity, distance from gates, kiosk and service points. Data collection and interpretation may provide the stimulus for environmental assessment or problem-solving activities (see Chapter 7).

6. Investigating the links
Take photographs to record the seasonal variation and patterns of growth. Then get the children to investigate the links between weather, temperature and seasonal changes. Ask them to look at the distribution of fallen leaves, seeds and nuts in relation to wind direction, spring growth, sunlight or shelter, animal or bird tracks in snow or the location of birds' nests in winter.

7. Where, when and how
Investigate where, when and how people use a park at different times of day or seasons. Get the children to use tally sheets and questionnaires or to interview their subjects with cassette recorders or camcorders. Ask them to find out why people come to the park, their distance from home or place of work, mode of travel, frequency of visit and whether they come on their own or in company.

8. Improvements
Survey whether visitors like the park or have suggestions for making improvements. The children could interview park personnel and record land-use activities associated with different aspects of park maintenance through the seasons. They could also chart the movement of materials or technical support within or beyond the locality, and trace connections between the local park and elsewhere.

II Cemeteries and graveyards
See also parks and gardens.

Cemeteries, graveyards and gardens of rest provide interesting, traffic-free places where many fieldwork techniques may be developed. Children should soon discover that much life goes on in such places of remembrance even if sometimes they need a hand lens in their detective work!

1. Gathering information
Encourage the children to record and measure the features, layout and character of graveyards using site plans, annotated sketches, drawings, creative writing or photography. They could collect numerical observations on simple tally sheets and construct bar graphs or develop a computer database. They could also go on to survey details of design, maintenance and wildlife conservation and use predrawn or enlarged site plans to plot well-kept and overgrown areas of vegetation in relation to tree height.

2. Environmental improvements
Plan for environmental improvements with the children and use fieldwork observations as a basis for a maintenance code which might, for example, encourage wildlife, new tree planting and seat positioning in quiet places. Ask the children to suggest ways of overcoming vandalism and litter.

3. Solving problems using hypotheses
Try solving problems and set up simple hypotheses: gather data and test to discover patterns and processes. For instance you could investigate to see if a relationship exists between the distance from path and height and variety of plantlife, or look for links between shade, shelter and the distribution of minibeasts. Investigate the relationship between weathering, direction of wind, or lichen growth and pollution from passing traffic. You could also discover if age or style of monuments increases with distance from gates or place of worship.

organisation of space offer scope for measurement and testing of acoustics, responses to sounds, silence and space or lighting effects. Outdoor site-work with the children could involve investigating weathering, mosses and lichens as evidence of environmental processes.

III Changing land-use, building sites and derelict land

Suggestions may also be applicable to fieldwork by railways, rivers and streams and disused quarries. Reminders about safety have general application.

Processes of change operate at many levels in urban areas. Although the most dramatic changes involve demolition, clearance and new construction, some buildings change use quite frequently. Detective work alerts children to these less visible changes taking place, as large houses are converted into multiple occupancy, or retail outlets change to office premises or residential use. Evidence of patterns of activity can be built up over time with photographs and children's work, so that future classes can compare building and land-use changes occurring at different scales.

1. Derelict land
When changes cannot be accommodated within existing buildings, structures are cleared away and replaced. Observe derelict buildings from a safe distance with the children and get them to suggest possible reasons for their present condition, clues to their former significance and possible future uses. Without even venturing on-

4. Weathering
Ask the children to locate specific features of the site using coordinates or compass directions. Get them to record evidence of weathering upon stone and architectural or monumental detail in relation to site and physical conditions. Alternatively, explore this aspect with the children through art, poetry or secondary research about rocks and origins of building styles.

5. Database
Get the children to compile a database from inscription evidence: names, dates, family size, life expectancy, occupations and population movements. Study the information with the children, which may reveal patterns of human activity and mobility through time.

6. Cross-curricular work
Many possibilities exist for you to bring in cross-curricular follow-up work. You will find many links with historical investigation and number work and opportunities for creative writing and science. Comparisons with tombs and burial customs in the past foster positive attitudes towards such sites, and cross-cultural explorations provide opportunities for the children to investigate belief systems and attitudes among different peoples. Using such sites clearly requires sensitivity to children's experiences and circumstances, but for many schools they represent a neglected resource for environmental fieldwork.

You could extend the fieldwork to consider related buildings, religious practice and spread of belief. Ask the children to investigate where different places of worship are located in a particular area and if there have been any changes in usage. On-site work with the children could involve gathering information on age, building material, structure and style, religious affiliation, size, attendance and distance travelled by worshippers. Internal dimensions and

site, you can get the children to draw detailed sketches from a safe vantage point and use large scale site plans to help them to consider wider processes of environmental change.

2. Demolition sites
Authorised access to a demolition site or land awaiting redevelopment can be very exciting for children. It is essential that you wear protective clothing and go with an official guide. Use site plans for the children to record evidence of former activity, building materials and environmental change. Get them to plot plant and wildlife distribution and then investigate patterns of natural regeneration on disturbed land. You could get the children to relate vegetation to damp and dry, warm or cool, exposed or sheltered areas and other physical aspects of the site; follow-up work can trace these species to places of origin and consider why they occur in particular sites.

3. Recolonisation of derelict land
Nature's recolonisation of derelict land and other urban wildlife activity is often to be found in unsuitable fieldwork locations. Authorised visits must stress the potential dangers; you may wish to avoid such sites altogether, even though a school visit might discourage the children from venturing alone into such tabooed places. A similar dilemma occurs over railway banks and fieldwork; full of hazards and fascination to young children, such visits must be undertaken only in safe circumstances. Ensure that the children observe and record from a safe distance, on

a station platform or even from a slow-moving train. Canal banks may likewise offer considerable fieldwork potential but you should also approach these with extreme caution.

4. Construction sites
You could take the children to visit a construction site, to see how the walls and foundations of a building in outline form evolve into a complete structure. Trace, with the children, the development of a building from its initial pegged-out ground plan to completion over a period of time. This process emphasises the relationship between an outline plan and its three-dimensional form, and provides a real example for you to compare with the box-modelling activity in Chapter 1 (page 11). This will also help the children to get more out of visits to historical sites where buildings survive only in outline form.

Some construction sites might facilitate soil investigation particularly where down-cutting for foundations provides a clear profile of different levels or strata. Analysing soil samples with the children takes on meaning if they have the chance to study soil in situ (see Chapter 5). Get them to spot where water gathers at lower levels and ask them to identify some simple patterns of drainage; a visit after heavy rain provides an excellent (if rather muddy) demonstration of water on sand, gravel and other exposed surfaces. Back in school you could try some modelling exercises with a sand tray; this takes on new significance when it has been vividly demonstrated in another situation.

Get the children to record building materials and their places of origin. Plot supply

lines and service points onto site plans and consider various aspects of design. Discuss how planning decisions need to consider choice and suitability of site for intended use, access and effects on nearby community or locality. Interview site personnel, planners or landscapers and find out about other people's work and underlying decision-making processes. Focus on recording and responding to colours, textures, patterns, shapes or sounds with younger children and meet people whose occupations gives insight into the adult world of work.

IV Stations, depots and ports

Suitable also for road traffic surveys and (with some modification) to regional airports and coastal ports and harbours. Passenger movement details may also be relevant for visitor surveys to recreational and leisure sites.

Planned opportunities to visit places where children can investigate people and goods on the move, gain value as the range and variety of their travel experiences expands. Whether going to a local bus depot or an international travel centre, children can consider who, how, when, what, where and why goods and people move, although the scale of activity and the range of enquiry will obviously vary from place to place.

1. Movement of people and goods

Get small groups of children to observe, count and record travel details on tally sheets or make sketches and impressionistic notes; while other groups might observe vehicles, containers, timetables or people passing a certain point in a given period to find out about flows of movement.

Some groups could look at information on ticket sales or handling of freight which could be obtained by interviews or questionnaires. Get them to gather the oral data systematically, using pre-drawn recording sheets or short questionnaires, to minimise the disruption (as answers depend on the good will of respondents).

Other groups could collect information about the travelling public or the staff. Get them to design questionnaires which seek information such as: approximate age, gender, number in group, amount of luggage, starting point and destination, one-way or return visit, other means of travel during journey, journey-time and frequency, duration of stay, reason for visit, or whether services are provided for disabled or very young unaccompanied travellers. Ask them to keep questions to a minimum during interviews and concentrate on aspects which offer an insight into how the travel centre operates or how travel and work patterns vary during different times of the day or year.

Finally, some children could gather data on the movement of goods. Questions might focus on different types of goods, routes and change-over points, journey times and frequency of service. Ask the children to find out whether certain items such as livestock and fresh flowers might need extra protection during transit.

2. How the site functions

Ask the children to use outline ground plans to record evidence of activities in different parts of the site and from this produce a land-use plan. They should record specialised vocabulary related to site functions on labelled sketches. Then ask them to chart the route of a passenger or freight container from arrival to departure point on pre-drawn flow diagrams. Capture more impressionistic responses to the character of the site in creative writing or quick sketches (which could be developed later). Encourage them to record evidence of sounds, smells, atmosphere, movement, building design, colour, signs and symbols, patterns and textures as stimuli for subsequent work.

3. Improving the site
Real or imaginary proposals for expansion, site improvement or closure might provide impetus for opinion surveys, site appraisals or design opportunities. The

children's observations will supplement the use of maps, newspapers, interviews and a range of other sources of evidence. You could get the children to investigate ways to improve site access, passenger facilities, sign-posting, information availability, car parking or landscaping. This new insight into places and processes will benefit both experienced young travellers and those children who have not had travel opportunities.

V Fieldwork and shopping
This is also suitable for retailing activities in railway stations, airports or bus depots, and is relevant for other aspects of street work which focus on land use, buildings and urban environmental change.

Going shopping is a familiar yet neglected aspect of children's urban experience, and fieldwork can pursue a variety of aspects according to situation, age of children and overall direction of work.

1. Quality of the shopping environment
Visit pedestrianised areas or purpose-built shopping centres to investigate the quality of the shopping environment; its smells, colours, character, sounds and overall condition. Get the children to survey opinions about aspects of design and then ask them to find out what makes shopping popular in a traffic-free place.

2. Comparing adjacent stores
Get the children to classify and map the use of adjacent stores in indoor malls and precincts, and record the movements of people between shops or from different entry points in relation to the car park or public transport. Get them to compare the size of shop or frontage width in relation to the entrance, refreshment areas, open sitting areas and so on.

Prior permission should be obtained to compare frontages with service areas and when investigating deliveries, waste disposal, safety and other aspects of design and maintenance.

Shops or stalls under cover may be convenient places for the children to undertake questionnaire surveys and interviews. They also provide sheltered spots for counting, sketching or evaluative activities involving creative writing. Shopping complexes may have personnel whose insights into other aspects of store organisation and security may be valuable in fieldwork.

3. Customer behaviour
Get the children to record, classify and interpret patterns of customer behaviour and different shopping activities.

Interviews and questionnaires help to identify relationships between purchases and type of shop, frequency of visit, distance travelled, time spent shopping and numbers of shoppers on their own or in company. The children could survey preferences on types of shopping, timing of visit and peoples' likes and dislikes. Afterwards, you could ask the children to compile a database and even compare the results at different locations or in different seasons.

4. Shopping streets

Many similar activities are possible in shopping streets where the presence of traffic and less purpose-built design might also be investigated (see Chapter 6).

Fieldwork in rural settings

Many of the activities and techniques suggested for urban areas are appropriate for rural-based fieldwork, whether investigating a small settlement or aspect of landscape character and environmental change in the countryside. Only the scale of activity and complexity of observable or underlying processes will differ in many instances. This section will therefore concentrate on scope for fieldwork on farms, near waterways and at coastal locations. Refer to Chapters 4 and 6 for additional suggestions on human activity and Chapters 5 and 7 for further discussion of the physical and environmental themes.

VI Farms and farmland

Suitable for visits to national or country parks or urban farms.

Farms vary greatly in their suitability for school visits according to the nature of farming, aspects of site design or lay-out and inclination of farm personnel to accommodate educational activities. They can be excellent outdoor classrooms where the children can further their understanding of where food comes from and develop wider awareness about the lives and concerns of those who live and work in the countryside. Depending on the age, background and learning experience of the children, a farm visit provides a wealth of opportunities for generating new ideas or fostering awareness and sensitivity based on first-hand experiences.

1. Gathering information

A farm visit may be a child's first encounter with countryside, animals and people met previously only in stories, songs or pictures. Meeting the farmer, animals and equipment and exploring barns, fields and farmyards are important new experiences. Focus their attention on direct encounter and observation. Get them to record information about people (farm staff and farmer's family), equipment (tractor, combine harvester, bailer or milk transporter), places

(farmhouse, dairy, garages, storage units, siloes or slurry yards) and livestock or crops, and encourage a basic awareness about the farm, the countryside and rural life.

For older children, a farm visit may establish a sense of place, raise awareness of the farmer as decision-maker and emphasise the role of a working farm in the modern countryside. Depending on their ability, you can involve them in sketches, questionnaires, interviews, camera work, measuring, plotting and mapping, trail following or field walking, sampling and note-taking from vantage points around the farm site.

2. Problem-solving
Use the information the children have gathered for problem-solving. Alert them to specific issues, such as safety, mechanisation, land-use and site design. Discuss with the children the farmer's working year, annual crop(s) or livestock and seasonal cycles Investigate wider aspects of farm and countryside management, nature and landscape conservation, animal welfare and agricultural change.

3. Land use and field size
Get the children to compare their records of different land-uses and field sizes in relation to physical features, including drainage, soil, aspect, height and slope. Use large-scale maps and site plans to get the children to discover the influence of distance from farm, road access and water source upon land use and field size. Get them to compare existing field boundaries with earlier maps and encourage them to look for evidence which shows changing field-size through time.

4. Pathways and rights-of-way
Get the children to identify pathways and rights of way, and look at different kinds of farm stiles in different areas. Get them to check whether any of the routes vary from those shown on the maps or aerial photographs. They could also record the effects of trespassing, crop trampling and free-roaming livestock, and link visual evidence to how those who visit or live and work in rural areas might view such countryside matters. Some children could investigate areas of conflict between farmers, ramblers, cyclists and so on and draw upon first-hand experiences and interviews.

5. Environmental issues
Some of the children could examine the role of windbreaks and hedgerows; this might also lead on to discussion of nature conservation, tree-planting and wider issues of alternative uses for farmland in periods of surplus production (various environmental issues are considered further in Chapter 7).

VII Streams, rivers and ponds
Suitable also for visits to coastal areas, wetlands, canals and lakes or reservoirs (with modification.

Many fieldwork opportunities exist within the study of rivers, streams, wetlands or coastal locations, and should be selected according to the overall focus of study, needs and background of the children. This section will focus on streams, since they provide relatively safe locations where children can investigate aspects of drainage, water quality, wildlife and human activity. Similar issues and techniques will be appropriate at other sites close to water.

1. Measuring the stream

Get the children to measure the speed, width and depth of the stream in small groups, using standard or non-standard units, and test for temperature variation in shallow and deeper parts of the channel. Then ask them to collect, sort, measure and compare the materials of stream bed or bank and on inner or outer curves.

2. Water quality

Get the children to test for water quality using appearance and smell, or look for plant life and the presence of minibeasts or micro-organisms in the water. Collect stream samples from other water sources and get them to compare the colour, sediment and organic content. Filter the water samples through different substances and get them to discuss the results. Investigate with the children how water quality may be influenced by the stream's source, direction of flow, seasonal change, adjacent land-uses and human activity.

3. Soil investigation

The banks of streams often show clear soil profiles where children can investigate soil in situ before taking samples for follow-up work in school. Encourage the children to measure different soil levels and then record variations in depth, thickness, colour and texture. Ask them to record the presence or absence of roots, moisture and minibeasts, and then discuss this with them and relate it to animal holes and other evidence of wildlife in, under, beside or above the water course, and to overall environmental quality.

4. Channel composition

Ask the children to compare the stream sides and the channel bed, and get them to observe any differences between sand, silt, soil, stones or pebbles and rocks. Ask them to look, feel, smell and handle different materials on-site. Get them to gather or record stones and pebbles according to shape, size, texture, colour or location in stream for later investigation and identification.

5. Erosion and weathering

Sites close to flowing water may offer clear examples of erosion and weathering processes which the children can measure, sketch and compare along the stream course. Encourage them to investigate simple relationships between weathering and speed of water, plant cover, soil, ground surface, and proximity to path or animal route. Get them to observe clues such as trickling soil, moving suspended materials, or crumbling banks which might indicate weathering processes at work. Repeated visits to a site and careful monitoring through time may build up databases which could illustrate longer term weathering processes.

6. Plant life

Plants growing in or adjacent to areas of water provide opportunities to consider the effects of drainage, flooding, soil depth or quality, sunlight, shelter and human activity. Suggest that the children compare numbers of species in contrasting locations with the distance from or along the banks of a stream, using a quadrat survey. Precise observation and detailed recording will enable the children to calculate and account for the density of species at different sites or the

changes over distance. They could link their findings to other physical aspects of the stream's situation.

7. Pollution
Streams have an unfortunate tendency to become unofficial dumps or sites of wind-blown refuse, so fieldwork may draw attention to problems of pollution and environmental management (which are discussed in Chapter 7). A pond or canal may offer similar opportunities for fieldwork, when access to flowing water is not readily available. Opportunities to discover other links between landscape, physical landform and different aspects of water are suggested in Chapter 5.

8. Cross-curricular links
Fieldwork in streams, rivers and ponds should offer opportunities for listening to the sounds the water makes, watching light and reflections, and looking for the colours, patterns and shapes of stones and plants. The children will find different meanings through creative responses using cross-curricular approaches, which will stimulate interest and deepen environmental awareness. (Fieldwork links with other subject areas are discussed further in Chapters 11 and 12.)

VIII Sea and seashore
Built-up sections of coastline will offer opportunities for varied forms of urban fieldwork; less developed coastal locations may have a variety of landforms and rural or semi-wild landscapes which might borrow approaches suggested in earlier sections on streams and farms.

Opportunities to investigate physical features and aspects of human activity exist in many coastal locations. Land-based investigation is emphasised here but, where circumstances permit and prior permission is obtained, off-shore experience by boat will offer an extra dimension to looking at the shore and gaining some sense of the sea. If you are reluctant to leave the shore, piers, promontories and spits will offer the next best vantage point for setting the shoreline in its wider context. Although the seashore is unique in being a meeting place for land and sea, and its lifeforms have adapted ingeniously to the regular exposures to salt water and fresh air, aspects can be examined just like their inland counterparts, while always keeping a watch on the tide!

1. Streams and rock-pools
Streams and rock-pools are ideal spots where the children can look, record, measure and interpret aspects of the marine environment in miniature.

2. Cliffs
Cliffs offer an excellent opportunity for examining rock or soil types, as well as undercutting and other patterns of weathering and erosion. Get the children to observe and record how the different types of rock are affected by saline content, wave action and weather. Point out the harder and softer beds, outcrops of rock and weak points vulnerable to attack by the sea. Encourage the children to compare the appearance, character and features of rocky, shingly and sandy shores and give them different natural materials to handle. They can record sounds, or sketch, write and respond to the texture, pattern, shape, colour, size and weight of materials and the distribution of materials on the beach.

3. Shoreline zones

Compare the different zones of a shoreline. Ask different groups of children to gather the information systematically in different areas: look at the top of the shore where storms periodically drench the splash zone or investigate at, in between and below the high and low tide marks. Each area is a distinctive habitat with its own special features, animals and plants, and there is constantly changing evidence of physical forms and seashore life.

4. Clues to wave movements

Look at ripple marks, sand texture, boulder and pebble size and beach materials as clues to wave movements and water patterns against rocks and shore. The children could also plot the distribution of flora and fauna or salt lines over rocks, shore and cliffs.

5. Marine pollution

Record flotsam and jetsam along high tide marks and classify other forms of litter as part of an enquiry into marine pollution. The children could collect water samples to test for salinity, suspended materials or buoyancy and 'feel'. They could also record colour, clarity, reflections and temperature for each sampling site.

6. Wind and waves

Watch how the wind affects the surface of the sea. Get the children to compare the rhythm of ripples or the glassy appearance of foam-capped breakers sending deep troughs and crests shoreward. From a safe vantage point, some children could use a stop watch to time the length between two successive crests. They could also gauge the approximate height of the waves against a known object or guess the waves' speed as they pass a motionless feature on the shore. You could get them to measure the time it takes water to reach certain points, to estimate the speed of an incoming or outgoing tide, and then highlight the dangers of becoming trapped. Encourage them to look and listen for evidence of air currents (blowing hair or voices being carried clearly illustrate wind direction). Ask them to look for signs of wind-twisted vegetation, piles of driftwood, dunes, sand and shingle deposits. Discuss with them the zigzag, sideways movement of waves and materials to create longshore drift and look for evidence on the shore.

7. Look at the horizon

Scan the apparently flat horizon and alert the children to the partly-hidden shapes of distant vessels; use this as evidence of the earth's spherical shape. They could also observe cloud patterns, including the gathering of clouds above land masses. You could then discuss these patterns with them.

8. Problem-solving activities

Direct observation of natural processes on the shore or at sea might lead to problem-solving activities. The children could investigate erosion and landscape protection, safety at sea and the seaside, pollution and environmental change. You may be able to study even wider issues, such as habitat protection, coastal development and issues facing those who visit, live or work on or beside the sea in some locations.

Reflections

Scope for fieldwork varies enormously from school to school and opportunities depend on the availability of transport, finance and also the behaviour and capabilities of individual children. Fieldwork experiences, whether a half-day outing or a week-long residential stay (under canvas, at a hostel or specialist centre) are central to geography and yet do not fit easily into narrow subject definitions.

Original research and firsthand encounters require children to practise and develop ideas, skills and attitudes which have a broad application to living and learning in and beyond school. Learning to be sensible and responsible for themselves and each other, their work, their contacts with other places and other people before, during and after a visit away from school is an essential part of children's own development and self-realisation during the primary years.
(Planning for this entitlement is discussed further in Chapter 13).

CHAPTER 3

Plans and maps

Maps and plans are integral to many people's lives. Mapped images in picture, symbol and colour surround us and depict many different aspects of the complex world in which we live. Produced in all forms and scales, from satellite images of tomorrow's weather through to floor plans of the local leisure centre, maps and plans provide many sources of information relevant to our daily needs. Clearly, maps are much more than tools for geographers, and children should be introduced to them from an early age.

Maps and plans are used in two ways: they provide information or can be a database for recording information. As the worn patch on maps in public places often indicates, maps can show you where you are. Being able to locate yourself on a route map, street or site plan helps to establish position and a sense of direction. Whether looking for a place to sit on a seating plan or a country named in the news or in a story or a holiday brochure, plans and maps help to establish location (where something or somewhere is in relation to other places, things or yourself).

Knowing where you are can help you find your way!

Maps and plans are useful aids for following a route. They may indicate how you can get from one place to another and what you might pass on the way. Moreover, they provide information about places which could make the unknown more familiar. Understanding what a plan or map may be able to tell us clearly depends on whether we can read its language. Once we are able to decode the message, a map or plan can reveal a vast amount of stored-up information.

BACKGROUND

Learning about maps

Children develop confidence and competence in working with maps only through practice in and beyond the classroom. Learning to use maps must therefore include opportunities for children to experience a map and the environment it represents at the same time. Map-related activities are, as a result, an important part of fieldwork.

Developing an awareness of where places are, what they look like, how they change through time, and what makes them distinctive requires frequent reference to maps of different scales. Maps enable children to place what they hear, see, read and otherwise encounter. They help to extend a child's locational framework and encourage curiosity about the wider world.

Mapwork should encourage children to become makers, users and readers of maps. When children can appreciate how plans and maps represent their surroundings, they are more likely to recognise how symbols can offer clues about less familiar places too. Children gain skills as they make decisions about drawing and using their own maps: which information to include and how to show it using words, colours, symbols and so on; choosing an appropriate piece of paper for their map; orientating their map or selecting a view point in order to find their way, and so on.

Recognising that each map has a purpose helps in understanding it. Maps can show particular types of information, be useful in certain situations or be drawn for different users. Reading maps produced by others becomes easier when these underlying reasons are understood. Issues of design, scale and clarity become meaningful when children use their own or each other's maps. The need to hold maps the right way up and read them accurately becomes relevant when set in a practical context.

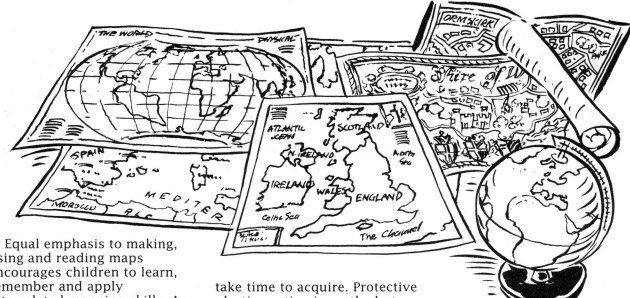

Equal emphasis to making, using and reading maps encourages children to learn, remember and apply interrelated mapping skills. As children use plans and maps to find or display information, follow routes and resolve real or imaginary problems, they develop skills of lasting value. Without real situations, mapping often becomes guesswork in response to a meaningless jumble of signs. Children should be encouraged to recognise the versatility of the map as a means to explore, find out and communicate about local and more distant places throughout the curriculum.

Maps and plans for classroom use

Schools should try to collect large-scale and small-scale maps which show near and distant localities (large-scale maps cover small areas in large amounts of detail while small-scale maps cover large areas in less detail). Limited resources often mean that maps showing the local area within its regional, national and international context will take time to acquire. Protective plastic coating is costly, but worthwhile, if children are to use maps regularly. Blank outline copies of maps and plans at different scales with simple grid frames are easy to photocopy, avoid unnecessary map-tracing and may be used alongside other maps.

A school map collection should include local street maps and town maps covering the immediate vicinity of the school and adjacent catchment area. Maps of different scales show the school neighbourhood within its local and regional setting. It is important to have maps which cover routes to fieldwork destinations and other longer-distance school journeys. Other more distant localities studied in detail should ideally have large-scale maps too.

The Ordnance Survey (or its equivalent in other countries) provides a range of maps suitable for investigation in and beyond the classroom. A map collection should contain other commercially produced, general purpose or thematic maps too. Varied examples familiarise children with different mapping styles.

Children can compare how cartographers are selective in what information they show and how they vary in emphasising different details and making generalisations. In turn, this will inform their own map-making activities.

Globes and atlases

Ideally, there should be a globe in every classroom. Globes are available in many sizes and different forms to show physical, political or thematic aspects of the earth. For young children, inflatable or stuffed cloth globes spinning through the air, with the occasional repair, are a reminder that earth needs careful treatment.

Inflatable globes offer flexibility and familiarity with the world through play. Non-fixed globes allow children to see and handle the world from different perspectives. They can learn to recognise patterns

of land and water, identify the shapes of continents and develop an awareness of distance, direction and position. Use of colour to convey information leads older children to compare political with physical globes and requires them to consider how a cartographer makes decisions about lettering, labelling and the positioning of symbols.

Globes can be used to teach children about the earth's movements in relation to the sun. A hand-held torch identifies areas of sunshine and darkness in different parts of the world. Folding cardboard globes or peeling an orange and laying the skin flat illustrates the difficulties of transferring the earth from a round to a flat surface and illustrates why the world is shown differently in map projections.

Cartographers over the centuries have made different frameworks of longitude and latitude lines in their search for effective ways to represent the earth in two-dimensional form. No method is completely problem-free. It is helpful to demonstrate this to the children by simple paper-cutting activities on a range of different blank map projections available for classroom use (see photocopiable pages 182–184).

The children can look at maps by early cartographers. Old maps can illustrate the way people saw the world in the past. Comparing maps from different parts of the world helps the children to appreciate how different people can (understandably) put different places at the centre! Collecting such maps could be part of a link with another school.

Using atlases enables children not only to practise reference skills but also to consider how information can be shown in different ways. Decisions on the order of map entries, the position of a country on a single or double-page spread, the use of colour, symbols, lettering, scale and place-names are challenges for the children as map-makers too. Critical awareness of how the printed map communicates thus links to an understanding of how, what, where and why information is shown in particular ways.

Imagery and mapwork

Photographic views of the earth's surface, whether taken from outer space or from a low-flying aircraft, supplement maps and plans in several important ways. Photographs and maps show different sorts of information. Satellite images and photographs show *everything*, so that the details may sometimes become confusing. Map-making, however, is selective and simplifies the information shown by using symbols. Thus many images from space and aerial photographs do not have to be decoded in the same way, and offer accessible ways for children to identify features, patterns, shapes and contrasts in familiar and unfamiliar places.

Scenes of earth from space are both exciting and striking. They are no longer unfamiliar to most children. Using satellite imagery in the classroom reminds children of the earth's beauty and fragility. Space images record continents and oceans, relief, drainage and vegetation in rich colours and dazzling clarity. They depict the world as an entity without artificially-imposed boundaries, which helps to illustrate how global processes do not stop at international frontiers.

Conventional aerial photographs, increasingly available in colour, offer an important source of visual evidence about landscape and land-use. There are two types of aerial photograph, depending on height and angle:
• oblique photographs offer a sideways view of the ground from a high vantage point which becomes clearer and less distorted with height;
• vertical photographs give a direct overhead view of features in plan form which enables comparison with maps, although again there is distortion away from the centre of the image.

Aerial photographs can come in a variety of scales and over a period of time. Some urban areas will have a series of photographs over recent years and these are ideal for investigating change. Individual photographs can cover relatively small areas,

ranging from perhaps an overhead view of the school site to a number of miles away. The area covered by a photograph depends on the scale as the size is constant. A photograph with a scale of 1:25,000 means that one unit (inches, centimetres, etc.) represents 25,000 units of the same on the ground.

For children, aerial photographs offer a bridge between direct observation and the more abstract, selective and symbolic representation in map or plan form. Wherever possible, a visit to a vantage point on a hill or high tower helps children to recognise this relationship. Even in the classroom, the fly on the wall perspective of the classroom in plan form can be replicated by standing on a chair!

Maps for floor and playground

Some commercially-produced maps and plans are ideal for

geographical explorations and play activities. Brightly coloured and hard-wearing, plans of zoos, farmyards and imaginary town or village centres are excellent for use with programmable toys or model trains and cars, to encourage following directions and using geographical vocabulary (see Chapter 10).

Some play-cloth or floor-maps are also available in giant-jigsaw format, offering further scope for physically fitting features together. Pegboard maps offer a ready-made base for recording places in the news, visits and connections. Generalised patterns of activity or aspects of the landscape can also be built up in blocks of coloured pegs. A link with a local secondary school might lead to older children making pegboards of local areas on which young children could record details or re-design places they know.

Physical and political maps of countries, world regions and the world are also available as floor-mats and play-cloths. Through play, children may familiarise themselves with the distribution of land and sea, shapes and outlines of continents and locate where they live in relation to other places. Children's inventiveness soon creates geographical versions of 'twister', 'hopscotch' and other games in which play and learning clearly combine.

Distortions and inaccuracies sometimes occur in floor-maps. Large-scale mats do not always adopt a uniform overhead viewpoint, so that buildings, people and lettering face different directions along the streets. Maps of Europe tend to represent the European Community countries rather than an extended Europe and, like other maps, have difficulty in placing boundaries to the region.

World floor-maps tend to be based on conventional projections and may thus be eurocentric and therefore need to be supplemented by maps showing other perspectives.

With a little ingenuity, street, national and world maps can be scaled up using an overhead projector and felt-tipped pens to draw around the projected image on large sheets of paper. More ambitious still, a lightly-drawn grid can transfer the school plan and neighbouring street network onto a piece of vinyl, which can be moved from room to room, or created more permanently on the playground surface. Ideally, a school playground should include painted maps at both large-scale and small-scale, to enrich children's play and to offer reminders about where the children live and the world around them.

Map sketches

All map-making involves selecting information. A sketch map extracts information from a printed map. It may be more closely geared to the needs of the children and a particular topic than other maps. Simple outline maps may be used for recording, updating, filling in details and creative planning or design work. Competence with pre-drawn sketch maps can lead to simple free-hand sketch maps, and later, working with scale. More sophisticated versions of sketching may be developed through using a simple art package, concept keyboard overlay (or other software packages) available for map-based activities with different age ranges (see Chapter 10).

ACTIVITIES

1. Getting streetwise

Objective
To encourage children to follow directions and to practise reading and using maps.

Age group
All ages.

Group size
Individuals or pairs.

What you need
A floor plan (with younger children) or multiple copies of a prepared street map, town plan or tourist map mounted and surrounded with a simple grid of squares and letters (ensure compass directions are marked and that symbols and street names are clearly legible), pictures and photographs, writing and art materials, reference books and tourist brochures.

What to do
Introduce the children to large copies of a street map of the area around school. Ask them to identify school and other key landmarks in the immediate locality. Encourage them to identify where they live, play and their routes to school. Ask the children to point out different routes from place to place on the plan. They should re-tell their route using 'left' and 'right'. Ask them to record their route either on the map using arrows to show where they turn, or in written form.

Further activities
• Discuss with the children how people give directions in different ways. Compare the use of such instructions as 'left' and 'right', street or road names, distances or travelling times and the use of landmarks.
• On a street map, record in colour how many street names and landmarks the children can identify in the local area, and ask them to name roads and landmarks (this can be interesting to compare at the start and end of a term or year).

2. Finding where you are

Objective
To familiarise children with simple letter or number grid references. To practise directions and use simple street plans.

Age group
Seven to eleven.

Group size
Individuals or pairs.

What you need
A large blank grid (see photocopiable page 187) so that you can add features, or a pre-drawn simple sketch map within a grid of squares with letter or number coordinates around all sides, enlarged copies of street plans mounted within a grid of letter or number coordinates, writing materials, tracing paper, plain paper.

What to do

Introduce the children to grid references as simple ways of locating information on a map or plan. Demonstrate how features can be marked and located on a map using simple grid references. Practise with the class how to read and use grid references by marking different positions on the large grid. Practise reading positions and giving grid references as a class or in pairs.

Once children have grasped the basic process, distribute street plan extracts (or simple outline maps) and ask children to use them to help answer the following questions:
• What are the letter grid references for...?
• What might you be doing at grid reference...?
• What might you find if you went due east from...?
• Where are you if you can see... on your left?
• Where are you if you can see... ahead of you?
• What is shown on this plan at grid reference...?
• Where are the widest and narrowest streets?

• Describe your route from... to ...
• If it takes three minutes to walk from... to..., how long might it take to...?
Children could devise their own questions and answers for each other.

Further activities

• Ask the children to follow a written description of a route. They will need town plans or street maps and should be able to mark their route on a photocopy or piece of tracing paper. This could be done in pairs or individually.
• Ask the children to sequence a simple set of directions which trace a route on the plan when set in the right order. They will need a map to help them. This activity might lead children to devise their own routes for others to sequence using a map of the local area or elsewhere. This could be also used in assessment.
• Discuss with the children how variation in shades of the same colour or graduated colours indicate depth or height, and where possible, compare pictures of named places to atlases.

• Spread out local maps and discuss the choice of particular colours.

3. Lost and found

Objective
To encourage map reading skills by searching for missing or hidden objects.

Age group
Seven to eleven.

Group size
Pairs or individuals.

What you need
Copies of large-scale maps or street plans.

What to do
Distribute local town plans or street maps and ask the children to imagine something valuable has been dropped during a visit to the town centre. Working in pairs, get one of the children to think of a place on the map where the missing object could be. The first child then gives their partner directions so that the missing object can be recovered. They take turns to choose locations.

Further activities
• This last activity may be adapted to other locations or involve the children in using maps of different scales. It could also be adapted for use with landscape photographs rather than map extracts.
• Working in groups with either maps or photographs, one child selects a place as a hide-away. Other children in the group have up to seven attempts at locating the mystery location. Their questions must be as precise

as possible in referring to features. Answers must be 'yes' or 'no'. Players take turns to hide in the map or photograph, and a scoring system might give the hidden person points each time there is a wrong answer, and a bonus if undiscovered after seven attempts.

4. Signs and symbols

Objective
To introduce children to ways of representing information by colour, drawing, shape, letter and symbol rather than by words.

Age group
Seven to eleven.

Group size
Whole class discussion, individuals or small groups.

What you need
Everyday signs and symbols, art materials, a pre-written imaginary description, a variety of maps of different scales showing a range of signs and symbols.

What to do
Introduce the children to signs and symbols in their everyday surroundings. Get the class to brainstorm signs and symbols found on clothes, machines, packages and in different places and draw up a list. Discuss why people use signs and symbols. Identify examples which children find easy and difficult to recognise. Encourage them to devise their own signs and symbols which indicate something about either themselves (a name or place label) or where resources are kept in the classroom.

Ask the children in groups (or on their own) to devise symbols to represent the features of a real or imaginary place. You could read a simple description aloud (presented as a written entry in a diary, travel log or message in a washed-up bottle) and then ask the children to locate the different features on a simple pre-drawn outline map or plan.

Introduce signs and symbols to the children on maps and plans, and discuss what they show us. Using maps of various scales, ask the children to identify different symbols and say what they mean. Show the children how symbols may be drawn as a plan, side-ways or in more abstract form.

Further activities
• Using a large-scale map, show the children examples of different types of symbols. Then describe a simple scavenger hunt or treasure hunt and ask the children to follow your verbal description from symbol to symbol across a map. Check that they do not get lost on the way!

• Discuss with the children how people see and interpret symbols in different ways. Ask them to compare their own symbols and interpretations. Give them maps and map legends to find the meaning of standard signs and symbols. Encourage the children to find symbols which may show things that are invisible on the ground. Point out how the size of symbols varies on maps of different scales.

5. Mapping colours

Objective
To introduce the children to the use of colour on plans and maps.

Group size
Individuals or pairs.

Age group
Nine to eleven.

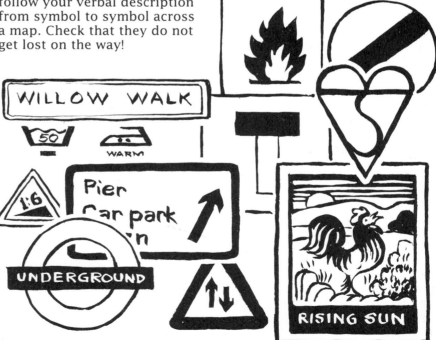

What you need
Pictures of different landscapes, atlases, information books with simple maps (showing forests, mountains, oceans, deserts), simple OS maps showing different rural and urban areas.

What to do
Show the children pictures which illustrate distinctive landscapes (such as deserts, oceans, mountains, forests and so on). Discuss with them the similarities and differences found in the pictures and identify landforms in different landscapes.

Introduce the children to simple maps which represent different landforms and examples of features. Ask the children to identify the colours and say what they think they stand for. Compare the maps with pictures of landscapes. Consider why scenes and landscapes are simplified into blocks of colour, and with the help of information books, record how colours may represent varied landscapes.

Further activities
Discuss with the children how variation in shades of the same colour or graduated colours indicate depth or height and where possible, compare pictures of named places to atlases.
• Spread out local maps and discuss the choice of particular colours for different features. Encourage the children to consider why particular colours might be used to show roads, motorways, buildings and so on. Some children might also look at how colour is used to show hours of sunshine or type of vegetation on other maps.

• Some children may be curious about map colours which bear little resemblance to reality. Encourage them to suggest any practical reasons for the colourful nature of political maps. Comparing maps with satellite images of the earth helps children to spot the artificial boundaries which political maps depict.
• Sometimes relief maps combine colour and shading. Discuss with the children how this gives a three-dimensional form to a flat surface. You could illustrate the effect of shadows and map shading by shining a torch across a simple landscape model.

6. Geo words

Objective
To establish the convention of using different symbols and styles of lettering to show different features on a map. To learn to orientate a map correctly at the start of a walk in the local area.

Age group
Seven to eleven

Group size
Individuals, small groups and whole class.

What you need
Selection of maps and atlases, recording sheets, small obstacles, writing materials, paper, outline sketch plans.

What to do
Discuss with the children how maps show different kinds of information. Ask them to identify how a cartographer shows information by colour, patterns, shading, pictures and words, letters or numbers. Once they can spot this, focus on the different ways of showing information one at a time. Encourage the children to look for different types of lettering on the map and how

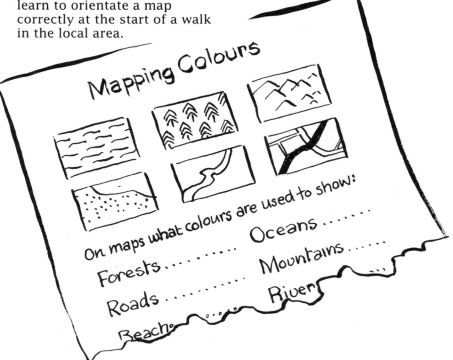

words are positioned. Ask them to identify which labels are shown in small letters or in capitals, light or bold print or in italics. Use a recording sheet to mark down the different ways information can be shown.

Then set up a simple obstacle route in the playground or plan a route in the local area of the school. Give the children outline sketch plans which show the route and mark the direction of north. Ask the children to orientate their plans correctly as they follow the route from point to point. Ask them to write in what they find at different points. Discuss in the classroom why maps and plans print writing the same way up and tell them about the convention of 'north' being at the top of a map. Compare their working sketches with standardised maps.

7. Place words

Objective
To compare variations in place names in different atlases.

Age group
Nine to eleven.

Group size
Individuals or small groups.

What you need
Variety of maps and atlases showing place-names in different languages, photocopiable page 188, writing materials, paper.

What to do
Discuss with the children the variety of languages spoken in the world. Ask them to identify which major languages are spoken in different countries (and in the local area). Introduce the children to examples of place names (such as capital cities) in different languages and use different atlases to find examples of names written in different

ways. Get the children to compile lists of names in different languages and then classify them according to city and country using photocopiable page 188. Ask the children to locate place names using atlases and indexes.

8. Mapping changes

Objective
To compare maps with reality in the immediate vicinity of the school, to show that they are never quite up-to-date but testify to processes of change.

Age group
Seven to eleven.

Group size
Pairs, although different contributions may form part of a class activity.

What you need
Copies of extracts of a large-scale map covering the immediate vicinity of the school, clean copies for classroom use, clip-boards, pencils, paper, a camera, historical maps, old and modern atlases.

What to do
Discuss with the children how maps become out-of-date. Ask them to identify any changes in the local area: focus their attention on the immediate vicinity of the school and ask them to brainstorm evidence which might indicate change. Discuss how they could record information on their plans.

Discuss with the children the route of a walk they are going to take. Ask them to identify from the map what they might see at specific

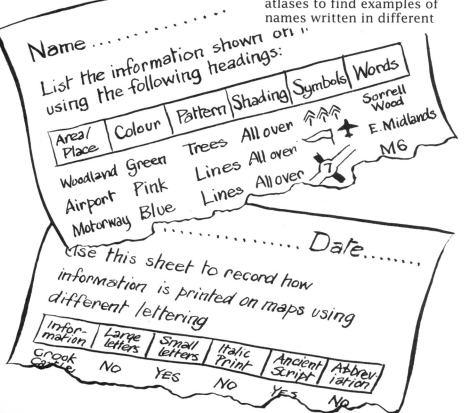

points. Divide the children into pairs before leaving the classroom. At pre-selected points ask several pairs of children to identify and record any evidence of change in that area.

Back in the classroom, team up pairs so that small groups can produce an up-to-date map of their section of the map. Join all the maps together and display. Discuss the types of changes noted and compare their map with historical maps or with other places, if appropriate.

Further activities
• This activity could be part of a longer locality study to show how observations of change in the environment can complement map evidence. Work might include gathering materials, photographs and tape recordings of local residents' comments on changes in the past and possible changes in the future.
• Discuss with the children photocopied examples of historical maps which show cartographers' changing perceptions of the shape of

continents. Ask the children to compare these maps with modern ones. In some localities, there may be physical features (such as rivers or lakes) which have changed shape since they were first mapped. Children can also compare names or boundaries on old and new atlases. (Atlases dating to when their parents or grandparents were at school link the changes more closely to their own lives.)

9. Mappable allsorts

Objective
To show the range of maps and plans produced for different purposes, users and places.

Age group
All ages.

Group size
Whole class, group, or individual.

What you need
Tourist and information brochures, visitor and street

plans, place mats, tickets, in-flight magazines, bus and train routes and other types of freely-available geographical emphemera which show maps and plans, writing materials, photocopiable page 189.

What to do
Start this activity with a short discussion about how maps and plans may help people. Ask the children where maps and plans may be found and discuss how they are used in different situations. Distribute a selection of maps and plans from different sources and ask the children to sort them into categories using photocopiable page 189. For each type of map or plan suggest who might use it. Encourage the children to practise reading the maps and plans through simple questioning activities. Ask the children to suggest how maps and plans could be used in other activities.

10. Looking from outer space

Objective
To introduce the children to satellite images and compare them with maps.

Age group
Nine to eleven.

Group size
Whole class, pairs and individuals.

What you need
Satellite images at different scales, hand lens, writing materials.

What to do
Discuss how pictures of the earth's surface may be taken from outer space. Ask the

children to identify and locate continents, oceans and visible features on a satellite image. Ask them to look at colours and textures on several images and compare their responses. Finally, ask them to compare satellite images with atlas or map information. Discuss any similarities and differences with the class.

Further activity
• You may have some detailed satellite images of the area around the school which record land-use in different colours. Tell the children what some of the key colours in satellite mapping stand for and ask them to decode an image of their own area. Use simple grid references around the satellite image to locate features. Ask them to identify the major land-use activity where they live. Compare these images with printed maps to see if there have been any changes since the maps were produced.

11. Place names

Objective
To find out about place names in the locality.

Age group
Seven to eleven.

Group size
Individuals or small groups.

What you need
A range of plans and maps of the local area, class lists of home addresses, street maps, large-scale maps, maps of 1:25,000 and 1:50,000, a list of common place names, reference books, art materials and graph paper or a software database, contact with the local council to give insight into street naming policies in the areas of new development.

What to do
Discuss with the children why people, places and streets have names. Distribute class lists of home addresses and ask the children to look for patterns in the naming of roads and streets. Ask them to find ways of grouping names. This could be done by entering street names from addresses or from the immediate vicinity of the school into a database (see Chapter 10). Ask them to investigate any names which have unusual or historical associations. Findings can be presented as bar graphs, print-outs or in written form.

Further activities
• Where local street names have historical associations, fieldwork and reference to old maps or street directories might identify when a particular street was developed. The name, event, or place it commemorates can be identified in an atlas if it indicates wider connections.
• Ask the children to identify on a local map place names of localities they have visited. Compile a class list of places they can name. Ask them to identify similar types of place names and to classify them according to ending. Discuss any patterns in place names which refer to colour, people or natural feature. Introduce the children to types of place names appropriate to your locality and ask them to find the origins of these. This information could be put in a database. To develop this activity further you could look at whether particular place names occur by rivers, woods on hills and so on.
• Once the children understand how place names derive they might make up their own place names, starting from their own name. Imaginary names could be used in mapping or modelling a fictitious place, such as an island or unexplored planet. Artwork could involve making their own place-name signs. They could also practise atlas skills and investigate whether their fictitious names really do exist.

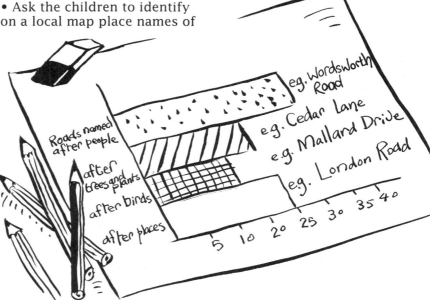

Reflections

Children become better makers and users of maps through practice and meaningful map related activities. Opinion about the best time to introduce children to maps varies. As people have begun to recognise map-using ability among pre-school children, older ideas about children's limited spatial awareness have required rethinking. Early learning processes involve many discoveries about where things are, way-finding and orientation. Indeed, these are part of the familiar experience of being lost. School must therefore extend these early experiences by providing systematic opportunities for progression.

Locational understanding develops from following directions, giving instructions to a programmable toy, using geographical vocabulary or making signpost maps. Next comes using simple compass references and grids of letter or number coordinates. Learning to follow and read directions involves using gradually more precise and complex references during the primary phase. Children's understanding of scale similarly begins with relative vocabulary (bigger/ smaller, longer/shorter), matching enlarged details to larger pictures, or drawing around objects to make outline plans on squared or plain paper and recognising proportional variations in their play and model-making (see Chapter 1).

Measuring may use non-standard or standard units and should involve work in and beyond the classroom. Children might pace straight-line distances in fieldwork or use tape and ranging poles; alternatively, they might measure distances on plans, maps or photographs with a strip marked into standard units. Either process involves children in gathering data which could be recorded as a scale drawing. Recording information on maps and plans drawn freehand or to scale, requires a gradually deepening understanding about signs and symbols, their function, design and problems of interpretation.

Maps drawn by young children which show themselves in relation to others, imaginary places or places they know, often contain disparate features, which they later learn to put in sequence and locate in space more accurately. Talking about what they have drawn helps to decode these very personalised proto-maps. As children gain additional map-making skills they may adopt more standardised conventions and produce maps for others to follow.

Sketch maps, plans to scale and maps of increasing complexity may be developed to display different kinds of information with or without information technology.

Primary children should become more familiar with using maps and plans of different scales. Using simply-drawn maps to locate hidden objects or characters in stories, to follow a route or to describe and record a short journey leads on to working with large-scale maps (either in or beyond the classroom). They should be able to appreciate and acknowledge the nested relationship of spaces and places covered by different types of large- and small-scale maps and recognise that maps have different purposes. Above all, they should enjoy using maps.

Familiarity with different types of maps and plans of a variety of scales is central to geographical understanding but should not be the sole responsibility of geography. Learning to use maps in and beyond the classroom is integral to many forms of investigation and is in part fostering children's curiosity about the world around them. Using maps within other curriculum areas helps children to see their wider application in making places accessible and understandable in terms of time and space.

CHAPTER 4

The study of places

The study of place fosters a sense of belonging and lies at the heart of children's emerging spatial and geographical awareness of both their immediate and other localities.

Many sources of impression and information may shape children's views of the world. Personal experiences, other people's experiences, stories, songs, television and other persuasive sources of image and message present children with a global medley of places and issues. The study of place helps to structure and systematise that awareness, and stimulate and sustain those interests and curiosity.

Childhood encounters with other places and peoples offer a basis for long-lasting perceptions and perspectives. From informed awareness should stem understanding, respect and appreciation, the means to challenge stereotyping and prejudice, and opportunities to explore patterns of diversity and interdependence.

BACKGROUND

Looking for starting points

Finding ways to give a first-hand experience to the study of other places is very important. Children's ability to take on notions of global significance should not be overlooked. Study of any unfamiliar place must be at a scale which is appropriate to the abilities of the children. Exploration of worlds elsewhere, particularly with younger children, should identify a recognisable place and ideally specific people.

Starting from the familiar and working outwards assumes that the local area can be better understood than elsewhere. This is not always the case, as local places may have many hidden parts, and other localities sometimes are easier to observe and understand at a distance. The concentric approach has been influenced by simplified versions of Piaget's ideas: it has sometimes prompted teachers to equate local areas with direct experience and non-local investigation with more abstract thinking. Clearly, the concrete firsthand experience provides a strong catalyst to the study of place, but with imaginative planning, it can be a springboard to both local and wider thinking.

Any comparison of localities (near and distant) should be rooted in understanding about real and familiar aspects of the immediate vicinity and community life. However, starting from the unfamiliar provokes the children's curiosity as it introduces excitement and novelty. It avoids travelling over familiar ground repeatedly and thus failing to reach the new area of study! Ironically, learning about the unknown often enables children to see the familiar through different eyes. Sometimes less familiar localities help children to recognise that many issues may have common roots and help them appreciate that some places, peoples and predicaments may be more closely connected than their apparent differences might suggest.

Selecting places

New awareness and knowledge should slot into a framework which offers a sense of where places are in relation to one another. Children should investigate aspects of their own local area, their home region, contrasting localities in their own country and other countries during their primary years. Their encounters with places, lifestyles and people-environment relationships should include town and country, rich and poor, as well as modern and traditional aspects in contrasting settings and parts of the world.

Care needs to be taken over the choice of localities. There should be opportunities to focus upon places (both familiar and unfamiliar) at a variety of scales through studies of particular localities, thematic approaches and specific issues. Flexibility to include localities in the news, visited on holiday or encountered through visitors, should ensure that places are met both formally and informally. No statutory requirement to teach about specific localities should deny children opportune encounters with other places too.

Questioning places

If children can learn to pose geographical questions which are applicable to different places and at different scales of enquiry, the locational framework developed at primary school becomes a stepping stone to future international knowledge and understanding. Basic questions should be transferable to any geographical setting although they may be expressed in different ways. Developing a sense of place might focus upon eight questions:

Questions of place	Rationale
1. What is this place like?	*This involves knowing where a place is and how it differs from other places. Children might consider why a particular place has certain characteristics and what makes it distinctive. They might investigate how personal, social, economic and cultural influences affect patterns of activity and contribute to the sense of place.*
2. How does this place compare with the local area and community?	*This requires thinking about similarities and differences evident in aspects of lifestyle, setting and people-place relationships. Children might consider who, how, where, why and which people live in a particular place. They might also compare living conditions and how people look after and interact with their surroundings.*
3. What connections are there with other places?	*This invites thinking about patterns of interdependence, and links connections between different localities and communities.*
4. How and why is this place changing?	*This raises questions about the nature of change and its consequences for different communities, lifestyles, habitats and environments.*
5. What do people feel about the changes?	*This alerts children to the importance of different perspectives. It encourages them to develop both objective and more empathetic approaches, and to try to see places through the eyes of an insider and outsider.*
6. What do changes affecting this place mean personally?	*This means being open to the potential meanings of any changes which might occur and being able to make a personal response based on deeply-felt or informed understanding.*
7. How are decisions made about this place?	*This prompts thinking about how individuals and groups of people have attitudes and ideas which affect opinions, decisions and actions in different ways. It alerts children to the influence of social, economic and political decision-making upon the environment.*
8. How might more be found out about this place?	*Children need to learn to become resourceful and to find ways of answering their own enquiries about the world around them. Developing investigative skills and learning to apply different sources of information and working methods are vital elements of primary geography.*

Placing places in the curriculum

There are a number of pitfalls to avoid when studying other places. Localities must not become a string of disconnected case-studies and disparate facts. A focus on another place should set localised details into an appropriate, wider context. Recognising the diversity of experience in any locality helps to minimise distortions through over-simplification and caricature. Comparative work should dispel narrow perspectives and perceptions. Tracing connections between localities and areas fosters interdependence, but should not identify places only as sources of products which serve somewhere else. Geography should help children to avoid gaining world views which are ethnocentric and problem-focused in their depiction of other places and lifestyles.

Another obstacle which may make other places hard for younger children to study is the concept of scale. Even though present trends seem to be re-defining countries into smaller political, territorial and cultural entities, the size of some countries makes scale very hard to appreciate. Distances, journey times, time zones, changes in the physical environment, and social, economic, cultural, religious and linguistic characteristics may form part of the wider context for a focused study of a specific locality or community.

Recognising that they live in more than one place at the same time can be confusing to some children. Understanding that they may live in a village or town and within a region, and also be part of a country involves abstract thinking. As children grasp the relationship of these nested places, their fascination with locating themselves precisely is often apparent.

Developing an understanding of people-place relationships should enable children to cook, sing, dance, paint, make, dress-up, role play, debate, measure, build, design, map and journey their way into issues, themes, lifestyles and environments in other parts of the world. Indeed all of these activities help to give children at different levels a meaningful sense of place. Combining the power of the imagination with informed understanding is central in making the study of distant places effective and memorable.

ACTIVITIES

1. *Going places*

Journeys can be exciting and adventurous ways to meet other places, peoples and lifestyles. Journey-related activities may be real or imaginary, based on fiction, personal experience or another person's experience. Whether set in the past, present or future, journeys require children to gather, interpret and apply information in different ways. Children's actual experience of journeys should not detract from these imaginative travels.
Additional ideas on journeys and routes may be found in Chapters 2, 3 and 6.

Objective
To encourage a sense of place through applying knowledge and understanding in imaginative or problem-solving situations.

Age range
All ages.

Group size
Whole class, and groups or individuals.

What you need
Ideally, travel baggage and contents for initial discussion, maps, atlases, plans, measuring materials, weather reports, news cuttings, travel brochures, time-tables, tourist literature, writing materials, reference books, art materials.

What to do
Discuss different kinds of journeys with the children. Then classify the journeys according to their distance, purpose, destination, time and means of travel (perhaps compiling a database). Use maps (or atlases) of different scales to identify the places visited by the children. Identify the key words and ideas for later reference.

Tell the children that they are going to plan a journey. This may be decided as a class or by groups of four or five children. Get them to agree on the identity of traveller(s) and compare the different travel needs for themselves, a backpacker, a head of state on tour, a sports team or pop group.

Get the children to decide upon their destination, length and purpose of visit, necessary clothing, currency and travel documents. Remind them that a longer journey offers the possibility of visiting several countries, crossing lines of longitude and latitude, the Equator, the Tropics of Cancer and Capricorn, the Arctic or Antarctic Circles or even time zones and the International Date Line. Encourage them to consider any stopovers on the route and the forms of transport they will encounter.

Ask the children to record and compare different modes of travel and alternative routes (shortest, cheapest, most luxurious, scenic, special interest). They could select a preferred route for detailed work.

Using available reference materials, ask the children to plan an agreed itinerary. On a map, they should plot the route, stopovers, and the daily and total distances. They could record the details of places and features passed or visited en route. Ask them to estimate the approximate travel times and costs for transport, accommodation and subsistence.

Ask the children to gather and map the climate, weather reports and other environmental information, so that they will know what conditions they will be encountering on their travels. (Data may even influence the timing and nature of the visit.)

The children could then research a route and destination and keep a travel journal. They might send (self-designed) postcards, or write a letter on the way or upon arrival. Other activities might include writing a letter to their prospective hosts (the children could tell them about themselves and how they would like to spend their time), writing a newspaper report of an incident, or writing an interview that they might have had with other travellers.

The children could map their journey in different ways. They could use symbols or pictures and secondary sources to identify features, buildings and distinctive elements of the landscape.

Finally, you could ask them to make a 'traveller's tips' leaflet to help others make their journey. They might include simple phrases and greetings, or practical details such as currency, weather data, traffic signs, festivals, customs and conventions driving on left or right.

2. Being in other places

Knowing where a place is and how it differs from other places requires close study. Fieldwork enables children to investigate their own locality; more distant places require using similar detective skills using plans and pictures. Tourist literature often contains many images which signal what is distinctive and special about a particular locality. Looking closely at landscapes and building design in an unfamiliar built environment can alert children to a place's character and offer clues about lifestyles. (Links exist in other chapters.)

Objective
To encourage close observation of another locality.

Age range
Five to nine.

Group size
Individuals or small groups.

What you need
Mounted pictures and photographs of distinctive localities, writing and art materials, a variety of maps of different scales, flip chart or paper for word bank, word processing package.

What to do
Ask the children to sort the pictures into different kinds of features (mountains, lakes, houses, markets, places of worship). Then compile the word bank to describe the different places and landscapes. Ask the children to write some simple descriptions of the places in the pictures and identify their likes and dislikes.

Suggest that they locate the places in the pictures using maps of different scales (including street plans or tourist maps). You could ask them to write a label for each picture and then produce a series of written clues which would assist with identification and provide a basis for devising games (or assessment).

Finally, ask the children to use the pictures and reference materials to identify the weather conditions of the different places they have looked at. How do these conditions affect the lives of the people in the locality, their work, homes, travel, leisure and food?

3. Gaining a physical sense of place

This activity requires children to gather and interpret evidence about why places are different. Starting from pictures and maps, attention focuses upon visible clues in the physical environment. It is important for children to see that lifestyles are not influenced by physical and natural processes alone. Environmental considerations must be set within a wider context of social, economic, cultural and political processes (according to the abilities of the children). Other activities which might be relevant can be found in Chapters 2, 5 and 7.

Objective
To consider how physical conditions (landforms, climate, earthquakes and so on) may affect the character of different localities and lifestyles.

Age range
All ages.

Group size
Individuals, pairs or small groups.

What you need
Street maps, town plans or tourist maps mounted and surrounded with simple grid of squares and letters, pictures and photographs, reference books and tourist brochures, samples of information on health precautions from local clinic or travel centre, paper, writing materials.

What to do
Show the children some pictures and maps of a different locality from their own. What physical features (hills, rivers, forests and so on) do they show? Get them to compare this locality with their local area. How may the physical features affect people's lives? Mount a picture on a piece of paper and ask the children to devise questions about what they can see. Swap questions between pairs and encourage them to answer each other's questions or add additional ones.

Give the children some reference materials about plants, animals, insects or reptiles associated with different localities (deserts, tropical rainforests, polar regions). Using pictures, ask them to suggest where different creatures might live. How do the physical conditions affect the life forms in different places? Suggest that they make comparisons with their local area.

Ask the children how they think people's lives might be affected by physical conditions in other localities. As a class, compile a list of hazards which may occur at different times of year (earthquakes, floods, drought, pollution). What, if any, precautions can be taken? What might influence the way people respond to hazards? How would they like to live in a place with these conditions? Then ask them to write a pamphlet to give advice to people moving to one of these localities (or into their own).

* HOW WOULD YOU DESCRIBE THIS LANDSCAPE?
* HOW WOULD ITS FEATURES AFFECT THE PEOPLE WHO LIVED THERE?

4. Exploring nooks and crannies

Since buildings are such a familiar feature of our surroundings, it is important to focus attention upon the built environment. Considerable overlap exists with aspects of human geography and geographical exploration in the immediate vicinity of the school. Further activities are suggested in Chapters 1, 2 and 6.

Objective
To focus attention on the built appearance of other places. To find evidence of lifestyle in the urban environment.

Age range
Seven to eleven.

Group size
Individuals or groups.

What you need
Prepared maps, town plans and tourist maps of the locality and contrasting areas (mounted and surrounded with a simple grid of squares and letters, with compass directions marked and symbols and street names clearly legible) with accompanying pictures, atlases, reference books, tourist brochures, picture dictionary, estate agents' leaflets, squared paper (for scale drawings).

What to do
Ask the children to devise routes of different kinds through a particular locality, using the pictures and maps (tourist circuit, journey to work, shopping trip). Then ask them to put in order a set of directions to go with a clearly-drawn map (see Chapter 3).

Next, ask the children to identify and classify types of historic and contemporary buildings, open spaces and the complex clutter of signs, street furniture, hoarding boards, seats and planters in the pictures. Discuss with the children how these features can give a place its identity; make a comparison with the local area. Suggest reasons for any similarities and differences found in contrasting areas.

Now using grid references and a local map, ask the children to identify the type (and whereabouts) of public buildings in the local area. Make a comparison with another locality. What are the similarities and differences? How does this affect the different lifestyles of people in these areas?

Ask the children to compare the design, size, and appearance of public and private buildings in a locality, using the pictures. Ask them to try to identify the building materials and other distinctive features. What do the buildings tell them about the physical conditions, lifestyles and cultural connections of the area? Ask them to make a comparison with the local area.

Encourage the children to use a street map to find different residential areas. Discuss with the children how a home close to an airport, school, hospital, health centre or in a quiet or busy part of a settlement or remote community might suit people with different needs and preferences.

Using pictures, reference books and estate agents' leaflets, encourage the children to design estate agents' brochures for a home in another area. They should draw a picture and then plan of the house to scale on squared paper. They could then label any distinctive design features of the house and describe it in a complimentary way in order to attract any prospective purchaser. Discuss with the children why the design of houses and other buildings might vary in contrasting areas, and why some designs may be sometimes similar.

5. Imagineering places

Objective
To find out how people respond differently to the visual character of places through creative expression.

Age range
All ages.

Group size
Groups or individuals.

What you need
A tape recorder, a selection of pictures of different localities from advertisements, tourist literature, calendars, reference books, art and writing materials.

What to do
Use the pictures and plans to help the children to model, draw or paint a distinctive building or feature in another locality. Draw their attention to distinctive patterns, shapes, colours and textures and encourage them to experiment with different designs using block printing.

Then ask the children to identify patterns, shapes, colours and textures evident in the appearance of their own area (or another locality if appropriate). As a class, create an image bank of different buildings or landscapes from particular view points. Discuss with the children the difference between natural and synthetic materials and look for intentional and unintentional patterns. Show the children how they can combine images, shapes and patterns into abstract pictures. They might record some different sounds to accompany the visual elements in their locality.

6. Perceiving places

Objective
To find out how people perceive and respond to places and localities.

Age range
All ages.

Group size
Groups or individuals.

What you need
A selection of printed pictures of different localities (drawn from advertisements, calendars, tourist literature and stories), reference books, survey sheets or questionnaires, clip boards, writing materials.

What to do
Discuss with the children the different impressions people have of particular places. Start with the local area and discuss how people think of and respond to it in different ways. List the likes and dislikes and try to spot patterns in the children's responses. What are their positive and negative images of the local area? What might influence the way they respond to a particular place?

Ask the children to survey people's images of different places. They should decide which places they wish to find out about at a local, regional, national or international level and whether they want people to respond to place names or pictures of places. Ask the children to devise their own questions. Discuss the results of the survey. What do people associate with different places? Which places are most and least known? Do people associate places with different types of image? Where do the images of a place come from? Ask the children to compare their findings with images in tourist and other kinds of literature. What are the positive and the negative images of other places? How does this compare with the image of their own area?

Finally, groups of children could make a picture montage to illustrate the variety of images associated with a particular locality.

7. Artefacts of place

Artefacts provide a direct encounter with people and lifestyles in another place and can encourage curiosity, speculation and appreciation.

Many kinds of artefacts are available; even holiday souvenirs can be used sensitively. Children should recognise that traditional and internationally available artefacts frequently co-exist in different places. This helps to avoid distorted understanding and stereotyping of lifestyles. Encouraging children to appreciate an object's value to its maker and the user, and understand its function in different contexts.

Objective
To use everyday objects to stimulate awareness of unfamiliar lifestyles and human activity in other localities.

Age range
All ages.

Group size
Groups of four or five.

What you need
A range of artefacts associated with everyday life or special occasions (made from natural and non-natural materials, new and old, partial and complete) which the children can handle with care, writing and art materials, information books, atlases.

What to do
Arrange the whole class in a circle and then show them one artefact. Challenge their detective skills! Without naming the object, ask the children to pass it around and ask each child to say something they know about it, using different senses (reassure those at the far end of circle). Encourage the children to think through various stages:

1. *Observation: what do I know about it?*
• it is heavy;
• it rattles;
• it smells musty.

2. *Questioning: what would I like to know about it?*
• what is it used for?
• where has it come from?
• what is it made of?
• who might have used it?
• do we have anything like it here?
• are there others like it?

3. *Finding solutions: where might I find out more about it?*
• where might I find others like it?
• who might know more about it?

Next, ask the children to write down any words or phrases in response to another artefact. Remind them to use their different senses when passing the object around. As a class compile a word-bank to describe the artefact.

Distribute artefacts to groups of children working together. Ask them as a group to inspect their object closely from different viewpoints, using their different senses. They should consider its appearance (shape, texture, design, decoration), production (materials, skills and effort), purpose (use, association, occasion) and meaning (value, significance) and so on. Then ask them to imagine if this object:
• could speak, what stories and experiences might it be able to tell about places it has visited or come from?
• is part of a lifestyle capsule, representing lifestyle and

behaviour in another part of the world. What else might be included to give an accurate picture of life and concerns in that locality?
• tells you about who made, used, owned and lost it?

Ask the groups to consider if they could:
• make this object using similar or equivalent materials?
• improve upon its design?
• identify how it might have a positive or negative effect upon its original surroundings?
• talk about it with someone who has used it or something similar?
• compare its meaning in its original and present situation?
• trace a route from its place of origin to present location?
• make a display which would enable other people to understand this object.

Further activities

For any age group, work on the study of places may lead onto a study of homes and lifestyles. Few places are totally uninhabited and where evidence suggests that human activity is absent or minimal, a range of other geographical questions about people and places become pertinent. Curiosity about the home-life of other people offers a basis for exploring the diversity and shared aspects of living in different places. Exchanges of pupils' pictures, writing and art-work captures children's perspectives about where and how they live. Such materials often have an immediacy and appeal which publications lack.
• Electronic mailing opens ways for rapid exchanges of information (using Campus 2000) and allows children to talk to each other on issues of

common interest. Access to facsimile facilities similarly enables the speedy exchange of children's writing and pictures (see Chapter 10).
• Access to video equipment offers a chance for children to produce materials which rely on image rather than spoken text to convey aspects of their lives and locality overcoming the barrier of language (see Chapter 9).
• Through fieldwork, surveys, interviews and questionnaires the children could collect material from other people and the local settlement to compare with another area (see Chapter 2).
• Imaginative work, role play and improvisation reinforce understanding of other places, peoples and processes of change. Newspaper reports provide eye-witness accounts suitable for exploring alternative perspectives and a range of issues. Montages of images and headlines may juxtapose contrasting views of localities and offer older

children a firmer basis for exploring the identity of a particular place.
• The children could cook and eat a meal traditionally associated with another place. This could lead to work on the origin of the ingredients, the people responsible for their production and the availability of these ingredients elsewhere. Surveys could explore preferences and reasons for people's enjoyment of eating foods from elsewhere. Authentic cooking utensils may be available, and it may be possible to set the meal within a specific context, to offer a sense of occasion as well as place. Older children might consider the cost of preparing a meal, and converting prices into other currencies. They could also consider implications for the household budget and family income. These activities avoid

AROUND THE WORLD

China

Paris
Antigua
France
Kenya
Holland
Venice
France
Paris
Italy
Switzerland
Egypt
Japan

WORLD FLAGS

STAMPS FROM AROUND THE WORLD

INDIA   AFRICA

• An informed understanding about a place (and publicity) could lead to the children making posters to promote another locality. They would need to consider what to include, omit and emphasise when choosing and arranging the image and text; this would introduce the children to the process of how localities have or acquire distinctive identities.

• Flags as symbols of national identity could provide further opportunities to explore meaning and origins. They offer scope for discussing and designing symbols for regional or international unity. The children could design their own class or individual flags, to express national, cultural, ethnic or other aspects of their self-identity. The study of national anthems could prompt older children to discuss issues of nationalism. Could the children devise a modern national anthem acceptable to all people?

• Stories, fables, folk tales, poetry and music offer atmosphere and magic to places. The traditional stories of some countries may offer clues about the past and may be of similar types. Modern stories may be quite distinctively different. The use of stories in developing children's sense of place is discussed in Chapter 8.

concentrating on producer/consumer exercises which could merely reinforce stereotyped views of life elsewhere.

• Younger children's interest in collections of labels, coins, stamps and postcards offer lots of possibilities for matching an object to a country (using maps, assembling picture jigsaws with named features, making simple games on the model of 'Happy Families' based on grouping collections of objects into specific countries). The study of different coins (or rubbings) could lead to design, language and number work. Stamps may provide an insight into the issues, concerns and aspects of a particular place. Children could design a set of stamps to promote a specific issue or celebrate an aspect of another locality.

Reflections

Investigative and imaginative approaches to other places and lifestyles enrich the study of place. They offer foundations for building greater tolerance, openness and sensitivity and derive from informed understanding, involvement and personal response. Many of the suggestions in this chapter are suitable for the study of any locality and region. They provide enquiry-led pathways to the study of place and could form either free-standing activities or combine into a geographically-oriented planned scheme. If these travels into unfamiliar places enable children to look afresh at themselves and their own locality, then the study of place will offer insights and encounters of lasting value.

CHAPTER 5

Physical geography

Some people live and work in places where the physical environment strongly influences their lifestyles and opportunities, while for others contact is more indirect. Yet, how we live and dress, where and when we travel, the places we visit, and what we think, see, hear, taste, feel and smell are all affected in some way by physical characteristics of the earth's surface.

As children develop, they gradually recognise there is a world beyond themselves. Children's discoveries about the physical environment should allow for mystery and wonder. This is not merely a world understood through facts, to be taken for granted; the changing nature of the physical world requires a broader response, where informed understanding and personal insight are based on sensation and feeling as well as factual knowledge.

Physical geography is an important part of the primary curriculum. Starting from familiar aspects, children should identify, investigate and interpret aspects of weather, water, rock and landform in contrasting geographical settings, both in and out of the classroom. This chapter focuses on three themes within physical geography and suggests activities for their development with children of different ages (further suggestions are in Chapters 2 and 7). There is scope for considerable overlap with science-based investigations and many links exist with creative writing, art, music and drama.

BACKGROUND

Ways of working

Many physical processes are best met through fieldwork. Practical opportunities for working in different kinds of physical environment obviously vary between schools, and even where visits and residential fieldwork extend the scope for first-hand encounters, nowhere is very likely to offer children direct contact with the whole range of physical processes suitable for the primary curriculum.

Through various indirect ways, less accessible aspects of the physical world can gain meaning within the classroom. Children can handle rocks, fossils and soil samples and observe, feel, smell, weigh, test and respond to the character of different substances. Sand trays, ice cubes, plastic guttering, watering cans and hoses may be used to illustrate aspects of weathering, drainage, erosion, landform formation and other environmental processes of topical concern. Other modelling materials make the construction of different landscapes possible too.

Films or videos from various sources provide dazzling imagery of contrasting landscapes suitable for selective viewing. (Globe-trotting members of the school and wider community often have untapped resources too.) Increasingly, the media provides up-to-date material on both long-monitored processes of environmental change and more irregular outbursts of extreme physical activity on, under or above the earth's surface. Building up these reference resources for children and colleagues over time will greatly benefit physical geography.

Meeting people who have lived in, worked in or visited contrasting physical environments offers personal insights which stimulate imaginative responses and make statistics and measurements meaningful. Capturing the character and essence of different physical settings through expressive work makes concern about the reality of the planet's condition more significant.

Looking for physical change

Maps are invaluable sources of information and also bases for recording data about physical processes. Fieldwork allows children to relate physical reality to the printed map or photograph and to record aspects of observable change. Whether influenced by a combination of natural or human agents, distinctive physical changes can alter the relief and character of the landscape in different ways.

Where physical processes occur at scales too small to trace even on larger-scale maps, enlarged map extracts, pre-drawn sketch maps and photographs are ideal ways to record and monitor processes of change. Building up sequences of scale drawings, sketches and photographs over time provide data banks for investigating patterns of seasonal and longer-term physical change at a micro-level. Newspapers, old maps, paintings or written accounts and memories can also provide graphic evidence of environmental changes within the local area. Travellers' diaries, ships' logs and other historical archives offer striking evidence of changing conditions beyond living memory, while clues in the landscape and rocks may indicate that the earth's surface and life forms were once very different.

Children can measure change over time and compare their findings with statistical data from elsewhere. Computers enable children to retrieve and analyse findings fed into a simple database. They might search for patterns in weather recordings or compare school weather with other locally-collected data. Spreadsheets and other software packages allow older children to collect, display and interrogate different types of data in problem-solving and predictive contexts (see Chapter 10). Time-lines help to display geographical processes operating over long periods and can be effectively related to rock specimens, building materials and imaginary views of how the local area may once have looked.

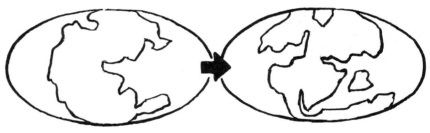

FIVE PERIODS OF LAND FORMATION

300 Million years ago

180 Million years ago

135 Million years ago

65 Million years ago

Today

ACTIVITIES

I. Landscape change

The internal structure of the earth may be compared very approximately to a peach. When cut in half, a peach reveals three layers. In the centre, the peach stone compares with the earth's *core*; the fleshy part around the stone is the *mantle*; and the skin is the earth's *crust*, consisting of massive 'floating' *plates* which collide from time to time, or ride up over each other producing those areas prone to earthquakes, volcanic activity and some of the world's youngest mountains.

The earth's crust consists of several different types of rock (igneous, sedimentary, metamorphic). As these rocks are formed and exposed to the effects of the elements, they are gradually broken down to produce distinctive landforms.

Objective
To introduce children to landforms and landscape change through different activities.

Age range
All ages.

Group size
Groups and individuals.

What you need
Writing and art materials, sand tray, landscape photographs and pictures, news reports of earthquakes/volcanoes/landslides, relevant nursery rhymes and poems, maps, reference books, atlases, different coloured A4 sheets, plastic tray or washing-up bowl.

1. Landscape features
Identify words associated with landscapes in stories, nursery rhymes and poems. Discuss some landscape features shown in book illustrations with the children. Ask the children to compare examples of physical features in books with local examples. Create a landscape which might bring together different characters from nursery rhymes and stories (see Chapter 8).

2. Landform processes
Model the processes responsible for different physical landscape features using familiar materials in the classroom. Using a sand tray, record what happens when a 'cliff' is undercut by water or when water flows down a 'hillside'. Model how sandcastles crumble away and compare this with pictures of cliffs collapsing, landslides or rock slides.

Relate these models to pictures of real examples known to the children. Locate places where distinctive and well-known examples may exist in maps and atlases.

Using pictures, show the children how layers of rocks can fold and tilt during movements of the earth's surface. Model this using a stack of A4-size papers of different colours. Press the papers so that they buckle or sag and ask the children to watch how the coloured layers arch upwards or downwards. Try to locate the pictures of folded rocks using maps of different scales.

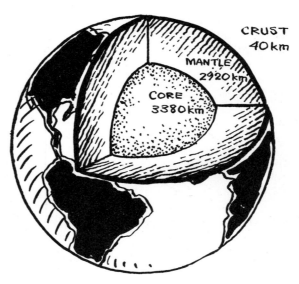

CRUST 40 km

MANTLE 2920 km

CORE 3380 km

3. Earthquakes
Locate places where earthquakes have happened in recent years. Give the children reference materials and ask them to research what happened and find out how settlements and communities coped. Use headlines as starting points for creative writing or improvisation.

Discuss with the children what causes earthquakes and where they occur. Make a time-line to show major earthquakes in the past. Locate examples on maps and find out whether any earthquake activity has been recorded in your area.

Model earthquake conditions. Ask the children to construct a model building or tower with LEGO bricks (or playing cards) using a tray or clipboard as a base. Ask them to test how far they can lift or tilt the base before the 'building' collapses. Ask them to record their findings and then try with other materials. Ask the children which materials stay upright longest on the moving surface. Ask them to try to design a house able to withstand a small earthquake.

Tell the children to imagine that scientists have predicted that a severe earthquake will occur in their area. Ask them to devise an emergency plan for the school or local community. Suggest how people and buildings might be affected and how they would deal with the different needs. They could research earthquakes in other areas to find out what happened on these occasions.

Investigate what happens when earthquakes happen deep under the seas and oceans. Simulate by rocking a shallow plastic tray or washing-up bowl partly full of water. Consider what happens to the surface and anything floating on it. Discuss with the children what happens when waves caused by underwater earthquakes meet the land. Try to find pictures of damage caused by *tidal waves* and *tsunamis* following an earthquake or underwater volcanic eruption.

Encourage the children to explore dramatic geological processes through dance and movement. Get them to discover the human dimension through news stories, eye-witness accounts or improvisations. They could improvise rescue situations appropriate to different types of dramatic change.

4. Local change
Examine with the children evidence of permanent and seasonal landscape changes in the local area using maps and aerial photographs. Show them scenes under different weather conditions and discuss what effect these might have upon the physical environment. Then identify how these landscapes may change in different ways through human and natural processes.

II. Landscapes of ice and snow

During different Ice Ages, *glaciers* and *ice sheets* scraped and ground their way over parts of the earth's surface. They carried large amounts of soil and rock. Materials deposited when the ice began to melt were often quite different from the underlying rocks. The present landscape in former glacial areas thus results from erosion attacking either the ice-scoured surface or the blanket of glacially-carried debris. However, the underlying rock is still deeply buried under a layer of snow and ice in many polar and high mountainous areas today.

Objective
To introduce children to landscapes of ice and snow. To make links with weather and human activity in icy environments, where appropriate.

Age range
Nine to eleven.

Group size
Whole class or groups.

What you need
Rock samples, pictures, photographs, media reports, maps to show glacial regions within different parts of the world, reference materials, tourist brochures.

1. Modelling a glacier
Explain to the children what a *glacier* is and where you can find them. Show the children pictures of glaciers and relate this to their own experience. Make a model glacier by pushing damp sand in a sand tray to give a bulldozing effect, or tilt a small pile of books to demonstrate the downward slipping of glacial ice. Discuss how these models are like a glacier.

Simulate the layers of ice growth in a glacier by freezing some water in a plastic container. Get the children to add successive amounts of water, making sure that each layer is almost frozen before the next is added.

Show the children how frozen water expands. Ask the children to weigh or measure the height of the water before and after it freezes in the cup. Put the frozen cups in different positions in and outside the classroom (or refrigerator) and time or monitor the freezing and thawing process. Suggest that the children examine the frozen water with a handlens to see the air trapped in the ice. Ask them to write about the findings.

Freeze autumn leaves or spring twigs in ice cubes and compare them with non-frozen examples. Ask the children to identify the differences, and then discuss how organic remains, including animals and human beings, have occasionally been found in glacier ice millions of years old. Discuss with the children how these finds could help us to understand the distant past. Tell them to look closely at the ice crystals as the ice cubes begin to melt. Compare this with melting pieces of ice which break free and float as icebergs in the sea near glacial areas.

2. People in glacial conditions
Ask the children to devise experiments to see why snow shoes, skis and sleds (motorised or traditional) are used in extreme snowy conditions. Some children may like to research other adaptations to extreme conditions of ice and snow.

Some children could research and write about rock climbers' and mountaineering expeditions in recent times, or in the past. If possible, invite someone to talk about mountain climbing in glacial areas from first-hand experience.

Discuss with the children what life would be like at an isolated research station in polar regions. Compare modern conditions with those of early explorers and researchers. Ask them to write about it creatively.

Show the children some pictures of glaciers and locate them using atlases, maps or satellite imagery. Identify glacial areas in tourist brochures. Where do people go to ski? When and why are ski resorts open in particular seasons? Ask them to search through the brochures for clues about how glacial areas change through tourism.

Encourage the children to find out about how animals adapt to low temperature conditions. They could make animal masks which show eye and ear adaptations.

The children could imagine that they live in a mountainous area where avalanches occur. They hear the rumble of an avalanche high up. Their home and friends may be threatened. Ask them to decide what they might do to prevent a disaster or how they would deal with the consequences of an unexpected avalanche. Ask them to think about escape routes, injuries and damage to buildings and rescue operations.

When appropriate, compare glacial conditions with local weather observations and relate this work to work on energy, materials and temperature.

III. Landscapes of fire

Igneous rocks are paradoxically both the oldest and newest rocks on earth and, as their name suggests, derive from the cooling and solidifying of extremely hot molten rock. In areas where the Earth's crust is unstable, magma periodically forces its way through points of weakness and appears on the surface. Children should recognise that landscapes formed by fire have happened in the past and also occur in the present in some areas of the world.

Objective
To introduce igneous rocks and the way in which they are formed.

Age range
All ages.

Group size
Groups and individuals.

What you need
Pictures from varied sources (media, stories, eye-witness or travellers' accounts, textbooks), news reports on recent activities, maps and diagrams, cooking utensils and ingredients, crystals (chrome/iron/potash alum, cobalt nitrate, copper/nickel sulphate, water-glass or sodium silicate), a shallow glass evaporating dish, thread and a large glass jar for growing crystals, atlases and maps, acetate overlays, writing materials and paper, reference books.

1. Volcanic activity
Show the children where 'landscapes of fire' can be found on a world map. Identify

Monday 17th December 1907
Today we can see very clearly. It is very quiet and still and the wind has died down completely. We will have to repair some of our equipment.

snow shoes and jackets as they have worn out. One of the huskies has died so it will be more difficult to pull our sledges over the ice – the other dogs are weak as it is. Food is running rather low but we are expecting a supply ship

any relevant landscape feature in the local or home area and mark it on a classroom geological time chart. Discuss with the children imaginary and eye-witness accounts of earth movements that have been in the news. Explain how volcanic craters, cones and lava flows form and the effects of ash, boulders and gases upon landscape and life-forms.

Ask the children to try some geological cooking in small groups! Use bowls of cooling custard or chocolate sauce to illustrate how molten rocks cool. Make different kinds of honeycomb toffee to illustrate the effects of trapped air in molten rock.

Show the children model volcanic activity under water. Get them to fill a large glass jar with cold water. Use a pipette to put a little food colouring or coloured ink into a small narrow-necked jar. Fill up carefully with warm or hot water and, while holding your thumb over the top, submerge the narrow-necked jar and place it on the bottom of the large jar. Remove your thumb and get the children to watch how the hot coloured water rises up through the cold water to the surface. Tell them that an underwater volcano would send molten rock and hot gases up from the ocean floor in a similar way.

Investigate how volcanic activity has created new landscapes in different parts of the world. Using reference books, ask the children to imagine that they have witnessed a volcanic eruption. Ask them to write a report for a local newspaper. Some children could draw a series of pictures on acetate overlays to show what happened.

Explain to the children what *active, dormant* and *extinct* volcanoes are. Ask them to research examples of each type of volcano and locate them on maps. Show them pictures of the different volcanoes, and tell them to compare the appearance of the volcanoes and the surrounding landscape.

Ask the children to imagine that they live close to a volcano which has been dormant for many years, and that one day they hear rumbles from deep inside the earth. They know this is a sign that the volcano will erupt: how do they feel and what do they do? Ask them to write about it.

In small groups, the children could research how people have responded in different ways to volcanic eruptions. Ask them to write about how people have tried to save their homes and settlements from flowing lava. What would they do?

Make a time-line of volcanic eruptions and list their effects upon people living near and far away. Ask the children to locate these eruptions on a world map and identify which other places were affected in some way by the volcanic activity.

Ask the children to research accounts of volcanic activity in contrasting periods and compare how the people responded. Get them to use recent news reports as a basis for writing headlines and reports about an eruption long ago.

2. Making crystals
Investigate with the children how crystals form when molten rock cools and turns solid. Grow tiny crystals to reveal how varied rates of

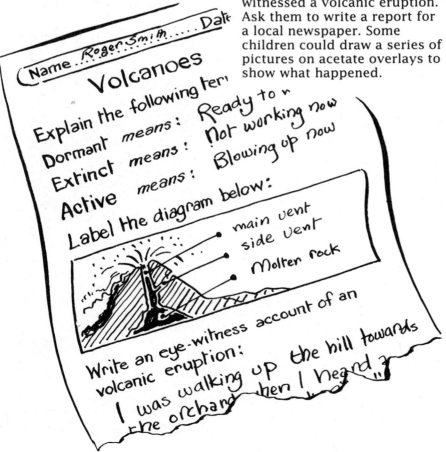

cooling affect the crystalline form of igneous rocks. Mix water-glass with an equal measure of water in a jar and observe what happens when different kinds of crystals are dropped into the water solution. Try other crystals using sugar, washing soda, lemonade powder and Epsom salts.

Ask the children to make larger crystals by mixing two dessertspoons of alum into a jar of water. Warm the water by standing the jar in a pan of hot water until the crystals dissolve. Allow the solution to cool, and when cold scatter a few more alum crystals into the water. Transfer a small amount of this saturated solution into a shallow evaporating dish and leave it until the liquid has evaporated. The children should then select a well-formed crystal and fasten it to a thread and suspend it in the rest of the saturated solution. Ask them to record how long the crystal takes to develop.

IV. Landscapes of pressure

Metamorphic rocks are found in the earth's outer crust and produce very distinctive landscapes. The rocks result from extremes of heat and pressure, which lead to physical and chemical changes in existing rocks. Much of the intense heat and pressure comes from deep within the earth. Some of the new rocks and minerals formed are highly valued by people.

Hardened by intense heat, some metamorphic rocks provide very strong building and roofing materials (including slate, granite and marbles). Distinctive textures

and fine crystals result from cooling at different speeds, or particles responding to heat in different ways, and make some of these 'new' rocks very attractive so that many people wear them as jewels.

Objective
To introduce metamorphic rocks and the way in which they are formed.

Age range
Nine to eleven.

Group size
Whole class and small groups.

What you need
Rock crystals and mineral samples, hardness and acid testing kit, scales, recording sheets, hand lenses, art and writing materials, cooking utensils and ingredients, modelling clay and use of kitchen oven or kiln, local map, reference books, atlas.

GRANITE

MARBLE

1. Metamorphic changes
Metamorphic changes are not particularly easy to imitate. However with careful cooking you can show the children how sugar crystals dissolve and reset in different forms as toffee, fudge or halva.

Bake and compare clay slabs in an oven or kiln. Ask the children to record their appearance, texture, weight and colour before and after cooking. Where appropriate, compare this with mud drying in puddles in hot conditions.

2. Looking at rocks
Survey with the children metamorphic rocks used in the building materials (e.g. marble, slate) of the school and found naturally in the local area. Check local monuments and tombstones. Use a magnifying

SLATE

LIMESTONE

glass so that the children can see the crystals and graining. Mark examples on a local map, if appropriate. Find examples of well-known buildings built from heat-transformed rocks. Encourage the children to look for any contrasts in the colour, structure and content of rocks found. Ask them to look closely at rocks where fresh weathering has exposed a clear surface; they should compare exposed and inner surfaces, and look for evidence of different responses to air and moisture. Tell the children that the thickness or angle of layers and cracks can be used as clues about how the rock was formed and more recent processes of change.

Small groups of children could weigh different substances and test for hardness using different scratching tools. Ask the children to list the results as they scratch each rock sample carefully with a finger nail, a copper coin, a knife or screw driver or steel file.

They should then enter the information into a database. Ask them to use colour, surface, hardness, visible crystal size, layers, ability to absorb water and texture to identify and compare rock samples.

Use pictures to identify landforms associated with metamorphic rocks and identify well-known landscapes and protected landforms.

Ask the children to observe patterns, structure, size, colour, transparency and texture in different crystal and mineral samples. Encourage creative writing and artwork in response to crystals and minerals.

Introduce children to precious and semi-precious stones. Look at their use in jewellery and how they respond to light. Ask them to name examples of gemstones and use maps to locate where different minerals and precious stones are found.

V. Landscapes of sediment

Rapid changes in temperature, chemical changes in the composition of rocks, and the continuous effects of wind, rain and gravity are *weathering* processes. The weathered rocks are broken down, transported and deposited in different forms to form *sedimentary* rocks. Water, slow-moving glaciers, sea and wind help to transport material. They continue the wearing-down process too, breaking up the weathered rock fragments further, and use these materials to strike, break and scour over surfaces they pass.

Children should become aware of landforms and landscapes caused through the removal or accumulation of sedimentary materials and appreciate how clues to past life forms may be found as fossils in such deposits.

Objective
To identify physical and chemical processes in the landscape through school-based activities.

Age range
All ages.

Group size
Small groups and individuals.

What you need
Soil, gravel and rock samples, fossils, glass containers, jars, trays, pulses, lentils, reference books, maps, pictures, writing and art materials, hair-dryer, rulers, sand tray, watering can.

1. Formation of sediments
Show the children limestone 'fur' deposits in a kettle in areas of hard water, to introduce how rocks are affected by chemical change. Relate this to pictures of rock formations in limestone areas.

Give a group of children different examples of sedimentary rocks. Ask them to compare their colour, texture, hardness, crystals, surface and ability to absorb water. Tell them to record the details or compile a database.

Ask the children to survey the local area for evidence of sediments and sedimentary rocks. (Look at puddles drying after rain.)

Test to see how certain minerals effervesce and dissolve in weak acid solutions, to introduce chemical weathering processes.

The children should record evidence of how water and temperature affect walls, pavement, monuments, paint-work and roofing in the local environment.

2. Modelling sedimentary processes
Use a hair-dryer over a sand tray to show the children how air currents move sand grains. Relate this to dune formation. Encourage them to compare the effects of air currents upon dry and moist sand. Discuss the life-forms that are adapted to desert conditions.

Use a hair-dryer and rulers to simulate sand movement in a sand tray model of a beach (see Chapter 2). Compare the effects of sand movement with and without barriers, and 'plant' other obstacles to show how the sand gathers around them. Link this work to different kinds of projects aimed at halting the spread of deserts (desertification).

Shake up a soil and gravel cocktail and ask the children to record how materials sink to the bottom of a jar and form distinct layers of coarse and fine sediment.

Simulate sedimentary layers being laid down through the use of different-coloured buttons, lentils and pulses in a glass jar.

Use a watering can over a sand tray (or hose water over sand or gravel) in the playground to show the effects of water erosion. A field visit to a beach, stream, builders' yard or construction site might also illustrate elements of erosion processes (see Chapter 2). Record what happens when water is hosed over materials of different size and texture in the playground. Spread out various layers of materials and observe the effects of hosing water over different combinations. Investigate how some materials move before others.

3. Fossils
Build up a classroom collection of fossils. Ask the children to devise a display on fossils for

a younger class. This could involve research in the library, museum visits, meeting specialists, model building and other design and interpretation issues. The children would need to apply and extend their own understanding to meeting the needs of younger children.

VI. Soils

Physical landscapes, contrasting land-use patterns and peoples' lifestyles are influenced by the presence, absence and quality of soil.

In some places, the instability of the earth's crust makes for constant uncertainty. In other places, the loss of topsoil, the build-up of silt or the advance of deserts threatens life itself. For all living things, soil is the vital link in the food chain. Understanding its importance, its relationship with the materials it comes from and also the various uses to which it is put, introduces children to important components within the broader context of environmental process and change.

Investigating soils is interesting and fun with young children. Ideally, an investigation should include looking at materials in situ and in the classroom. Any site-work must select areas where the ground surface (whether soils or rocks) is stable. The collection of samples must minimise disruption and avoid unnecessary removal of materials. Rapid rates of natural weathering need not be assisted by soil-sampling and destructive rock-hounding activity when fallen debris and pebbles can provide ample evidence!

Objective
To recognise some of the characteristics of different soils.

Age range
All ages.

Group size
Whole class and groups.

What you need
Spade, measuring ruler, sample bags, large and small glass jars, soil, sand, clay, seeds, pots, air-tight containers, funnels, filters, newspapers, watering can, telephone directory, maps, reference materials, local map.

1. Soil horizons
Find or dig a clear section through the soil in the school field. Tell the children to measure and record details about the depth and thickness of soil horizons or levels, variations in colour and texture and evidence of water, roots and other living organisms.

2. Comparing types of soil
Encourage the children to discover how sand, soil and clay feel, smell, weigh and behave when wet or dry by squeezing, moulding or trickling materials. Ask them to record the different characteristics (rough, smooth, dry, wet, sticky, lumpy). Explain that some soils contain more sand and others more clay and that this affects what plants can grow on them.

Ask the children to shake soil cocktails in some glass

jars filled with water. They should then compare different soil samples, using the same quantity of soil each time (colour, appearance, and how long the water takes to clear). Ask them to measure the height of the different amounts of gravel, sand, silt and clay particles that have settled at the bottom of each glass jar.

Help the children to compare local soil samples and examine their colour, content and texture. Test their suitability for growing mustard and cress seeds. Alternatively, take some garden soil from the surface and some more from about 45cm down. Put in small pots and scatter an equal number of seeds in each pot. Give the same amount of water, light and heat to the pots. The children should record how the seeds develop, then discuss what this suggests about the soil.

Mix soil with enough water to make the soil particles stick together. Form two soft round balls: put both in air-tight containers and place one container in the freezer until the soil is hard. Remove the soil balls from the containers and place them on newspaper. Ask the children to record what happens when the soil balls are tapped. Which one breaks down more easily?

Make some small clay slabs of identical size. Ask the children to measure them and leave the slabs to dry over a number of days. Ask the children to measure them periodically and record how their size changes. Discuss why the slabs shrink.

Ask the children to pour water from a watering-can at different heights and find out how soil, sand and gravel materials absorb water differently. They should compare how water moves and drains through materials in different ways. Ask them to time how long water takes to drain from materials in inverted jars fitted with cloth (or paper) filters. Which substance holds most water?

Put some soil into the top of a funnel. Hold over a container and pour a little water into the funnel. Ask the children to use a stop watch (or simply count) to measure how long the water takes to drain into the container below.

Fill three identical small jars (or test-tubes) with soil, sand and potting compost (or clay). Fix a small piece of cloth (muslin) over the end of each container, and stand it upside down in water. Ask the children to look for evidence of water rising up through the three jars over several days. Discuss with the children how this affects plant growth.

3. Sandy names
Ask the children to find names which suggest sands and soils on a local map. Types of soil and rock can be identified from place names too (Chalk farm, Sandy Lane, Marsh, Clayton). Use a telephone directory (or the school register) to find examples of surnames which suggest soils and sands. Which names are most common? Why do you think people had such surnames?

VII. Becoming weather-wise

Becoming weather-wise starts as children meet different conditions which affect how they feel and what they can do or wear. Extending this awareness builds on direct experience of variations through introducing new vocabulary and themes. Weather studies involve observing an increasing range of weather elements, learning to record in greater detail, identifying weather effects through experiments, looking for patterns and relationships and applying weather information to other patterns of human activity and environmental change. Exploring these dimensions of weather depends on first-hand experience and children's initial grasp of basic weather processes.

Objective
To introduce ways of measuring the weather. To understand the different types of weather and their effects on people's lifestyles.

Age range
All ages.

Group size
Groups and individuals.

What you need
Simple weather measuring instruments, writing materials, paper, recording sheets, music instruments, art materials, outline world map, atlases, seaweed, pine cones, ropes of natural fibres, weather maps, weather reports, satellite images, reference books.

1. Observing the weather
Discuss the weather daily with the children. They should become familiar with different conditions (hot/cold, wet/dry, sunny/cloudy, clear/misty, windy/still). Identify the importance of shelter, direction, sun and shade, temperature, rain, snow, ice and clouds on different conditions.

Use stories, poetry, pictures, music and role-play to illustrate different weather conditions and the effects of weather upon people and their surroundings in contrasting parts of the world.

Ask the children what weather gear they should take on a short outing. They should describe how weather conditions affect their different senses.

Encourage the children to look at evidence of the weather around, above and below them! Discuss how conditions affect colours, patterns, surfaces, reflections, shapes, sounds or smells. Look

at puddles, plants and the behaviour of people and animals. Draw, photograph, talk or write about observable weather conditions.

2. Weather patterns

Ask the children to look for weather patterns and compare data over long periods of time and between places. They could investigate freak or unusual forms of weather in the news and identify variations and patterns. Discuss how 'normal' weather conditions vary from season to season and in different parts of the world.

Make a world weather map to identify different weather conditions. Ask the children to record weather in different parts of the world over a week.

3. Recording the weather

Direct observation of daily changes in weather starts in the classroom and the playground. The children should collect weather data daily using simple instruments

and varied recording techniques to measure, record, store and interpret the information.

Ask the children to record the effects of sunlight, daily temperature changes and shadows in different ways. Practise vocabulary associated with weather conditions in spoken and written forms.

Relate wind conditions to simple compass directions (using weather vanes, wind-blown trees or lichen on walls and trees). Compare the children's estimates of weather measurements with standard unit measurements. Test simple hypotheses and use standard (rather than self- or class-designed) symbols to record weather findings.

Introduce a simply-made (or bought) weather testing kit (rain gauge, wind vane or wind

sock, compass, hand-held rotary wind anemometer and sundial). Introduce children to temperature readings, and how to use a maximum/minimum thermometer indoors and outside in different conditions. Record on a regular basis and share a weather report with the rest of the school.

Discuss traditional weather lore and measuring techniques with the children. Where possible, introduce seaweed, pine cones and ropes of natural fibres as indicators of weather conditions. Test and compare these methods with other ways of monitoring

weather conditions. Discuss weather sayings and country folklore with the children and compare them with their observations.

If possible, compare direct observations and weather recording with data from the Meteorological Office, weather maps and satellite images, news reports or automatic weather stations.

4. Weather and people

Weather work may involve visiting or meeting staff from a weather office or other place (for instance airport, coastal, forest or upland rescue station) where weather conditions are monitored. Identify how weather conditions influence the lives and livelihoods of farmers, engineers, and trawler or oil rig crews and that many other outdoor workers depend on accurate weather prediction and responsible action. Discuss with the children how people, plants and animals protect themselves against extremes of temperature or exposure to sun.

Apply weather data to local and wider issues. Monitor levels of traffic or numbers of people in the local park on rainy and sunny days or the number of outdoor sports events rained off in a season. Ask the children to survey how weather conditions and seasonal variations affect how people travel to school, spend their leisure time or plan holidays.

Chart how seasonal changes affect the appearance of the school site and local area, or the availability of fresh foods (particularly in the past, using old recipe books). Compare how winter and summer weather conditions affect people working in tourism, farming and other outdoor activities.

5. Climate

Where appropriate, set weather data into the wider context of the climate. Compare how climate and seasonal characteristics vary in different parts of the world, using maps, pictures and statistical data. Introduce wider issues of climatic and environmental change.

Discuss with the children how fossils, footprints and geological remains provide existing clues of distant climatic changes. Encourage them to research how some climatic changes are recorded in rock and cave art, archaeological evidence of plant and animal remains, paintings and folk memory.

Reflections

Many familiar experiences underpin children's developing awareness of physical geography at primary school. Children meet words which refer to weather, scenery and distinctive physical processes in everyday activities through play, outings, visits and various sources of text and image. Physical geography extends this imprecise and impressionistic understanding through offering more systematic opportunities to explore, analyse and understand the physical aspects of the world around them.

Around the world, there are old and new explanations of how landscapes, weather and different physical processes exist. They reveal a shared human need through time to make sense of a physical world which is at times very unpredictable. Newer interpretations of the physical world need to be balanced with an appreciation of earlier wisdom and belief, buried in folklore and oral tradition. Understanding the way in which people's perspectives alter and differ mirrors the planet's own history of physical change, and hints at how ideas and knowledge may differ in years to come. These constantly-changing ideas make environmental change both topical and challenging in the primary classroom today. The immediate and often inexplicable nature of global physical processes motivates and enriches the search for understanding in this area of primary geography. Physical investigation should spark wider environmental thinking. Acknowledging how physical processes affect themselves and others throughout the world in contrasting ways should strengthen children's notions of interdependence and shared responsibility for the survival and well-being of an extremely old and fragile planet.

CHAPTER 6

Human geography

Human geography surrounds us so completely that we sometimes overlook it altogether. Patterns of human activity and processes which link people, places, problems and possibilities over different distances and time scales are never far away. Many popular topics in primary schools arise from interactions between the earth and its peoples in one form or another. Yet often the geographical element is minimal or absorbed into another area of the curriculum. By recognising the geographical character in work with children, teachers are better placed to plan for progression. This chapter suggests activities which may explore key ideas in human geography in and beyond the local area.

Transport

Movement is part of children's daily lives. From very young, they are involved in moving from place to place and are aware of others coming and going. They may encounter different forms of public, private and personal transport, ranging from baby buggies to transatlantic jets. Sorting types of transport according to size, scale, frequency of use, appearance and likes or dislikes may build on direct experience. Recognising that people travel in different ways for different purposes may likewise start from the familiar. More complex notions of distance, time, cost and convenience and environmental issues extend early thinking and are assisted by observation, surveys, interviews and other geographical investigations in and beyond school.

Young children's lives are also influenced by the movement of goods, although their attention probably focuses most on goods such as food, clothes or toys and other things which seem relevant to them. Making connections between the goods at home, school, in shops, on roads, railways or at sea begins with direct observation, talking to people, visiting places and being encouraged to notice what they pass, or what passes them when they travel.

Key questions about transport might include:
• Who travels from place to place?
• How do people and goods travel?
• What kinds of transport are used?
• Why do they travel?
• How far do they travel?
• How often do people make journeys?
• Which places do people and goods travel between?
• What are the best and worst aspects of transport?
• How might transport be improved?
• How are lives and places affected by transport?

Communications

Communication involves passing on information, messages and meanings. It links with transport because both depend upon some form of movement. In town and country, children are part of a global web of communications which shapes their lives, experiences and expectations in different ways. Reports of distant events and decisions may affect what children eat, drink, wear or do. Soundwaves transmit sounds and rhythms around the world while images and text are beamed, bounced, digitised and otherwise transmitted from place to place.

Everywhere, communication involves people talking, shouting or whispering to each other in one of the many

languages of the world. The spoken word is passed on by recordings, satellite, cable or transmitter. Telephones at home or school, on trains or boats, in other places of work and pleasure carry messages and information over varied distances between different people at all times of night and day. The written word passes on news of personal and international level in letters, magazines and newspapers. Messages pass through information technology systems, including faxes, computer networks and modums, teletext, electronic mailing and so on.

Conventional forms of communication may also exist. Flags on ships, buildings or by the beach indicate particular conditions or events. Flares, whistles and flashes communicate warnings or messages from people in need. Smoke signals and beacons occasionally convey information, as in earlier times. In short, the desire to share information with others prompts much ingenuity in times of peace and war, and people everywhere have found many ways to communicate

ideas in picture, symbol, sound and other forms.

A landscape of communications surrounds us in the form of overhead wires, transmission cables, aerials, satellite dishes, flag-poles and letter-boxes. Sirens, bells, signals and voices also provide a soundscape of communications which, with careful listening, may reveal that birds and animals communicate in audible ways as well.

Key questions about communications might include:
• What are the different types of communication?
• How do communications vary from place to place?
• What types of communication occur locally or at school?
• Which places are linked by communications?
• How and why do people communicate in different ways?
• How are peoples' lives affected by communications?
• How do communications affect the landscape?

• What types of work are associated with communications?
• Why do communication problems sometimes occur?

Body language, gesture, behaviour and other forms of communication may also be valid for consideration but may be explored through other curriculum areas.

Work

Recognising that people may do certain activities as work rather than for pleasure is often difficult for young children to grasp. Understanding that their own lives are bound up with many kinds of work done by people around them is an important discovery process, and requires helping children to identify jobs and work-related activities in and beyond the home.

Work around the World

Chef in London

Carpenter - Wittu

Engineer in Zambia

Business-Woman in New York

Doctor

Farmer

Paid and unpaid employment by men, women and children involves many kinds of jobs or tasks, which together give character to particular kinds of work. Direct experience, visits and talking with people give insights into work which then often gain meaning through improvisation and imitative play, in and out of the classroom. Observation and surveys identify how people work at different times and for different numbers of hours. People may work alone or with others, in different settings, and their attitudes towards their work may vary. Appreciating these differences gives children a better understanding about the overall functioning of their school and other places within the wider community, as well as respect for the contributions made by others to their own lives. Key questions about work might include:

• What types of work do people do?
• Where do they work?
• When do they work?
• How do they travel to work?
• What do they feel about their work?
• How does work vary between places?
• How does work vary within a place?
• How long have people done particular kinds of work?
• Which kinds of work are done alone or with other people?
• Which kinds of work connect with other places?
• How do people feel about any changes which affect their work?

The world of work must be approached with care, and children must learn that people are able or unable to work for many different personal, cultural and economic reasons. Recognising that different factors influence whether people work or not, and that opportunities for work vary from place to place, is important in developing older children's understanding of the complex and changing world in which they live.

Leisure

The common human need to rest from work leads people to many different kinds of leisure activity around the world. How people may spend their time when not at work can be investigated by children using original data and secondary research in different ways. Patterns of leisure activity require sensitive interpretation, as findings may reflect considerable differences in amounts of time, money and commitment. Personal or family circumstances, cultural context, interests, mobility and setting may offer contrasting types of opportunity for leisure and recreation in different homes and communities.

Recognising reasons for conflicting leisure interests, learning to appreciate the merits of different leisure activities, and encountering recreational opportunities which may bring lasting enjoyment, are part of understanding how people spend their time, behave and interact with other people and places. Landscapes of leisure may comprise parks, playgrounds, sports centres and bars, while clues to less visible recreational activity may also be found in town and country. Realising that what some people do as leisure others may do as work, and that some leisure activities also involve other people being hard at work, are issues that older children might also want to explore in their local area.

Key questions about leisure might include:
• What types of leisure do people take part in?
• How much time do people spend on leisure?
• Where do they spend their leisure time?
• Who do they spend their leisure time with?
• When do people take part in leisure activities?
• Which types of leisure take place indoors or outside?
• Which leisure activities involve purpose-built places?
• How does leisure affect local people?
• How does leisure affect the local area?
• Could local leisure opportunities be improved in any way?

Homes and houses

Looking at how and where people live, offers scope for local investigation and comparisons with elsewhere. Children may focus on aspects of quality or quantity of homes and housing in any area at different levels of enquiry. They should see the variety of housing within and between communities as responses to a common need for privacy and protection. How people's homes vary in size, style, materials, character and quality needs to be related to the different opportunities for obtaining or constructing a place to live. Recognising that houses reflect aspects of lifestyle and circumstances, which may change in the life of a house and its inhabitants, helps children to understand the enormous contrasts to be found within their own areas and other places.

Once children recognise local variety in homes, the diversity in other countries becomes easier to explore without risks of stereotyping. Through pictures and stories they should meet the homes of rich and poor in town and country and recognise that homes, modest or lavish, old or new, traditional or modern in style, may co-exist. Appreciating that people may share housing needs, but not always the means to meet those needs, helps children to account for contrasting patterns. Realising that people may value the physical characteristic or domestic function of homes differently, or vary in how they identify essentials for living, also gives children a better understanding of how homes vary through time and space.

Investigating where or how a house is built, and how spaces within, around and between homes have different uses, identifies patterns of land-use at contrasting scales. Understanding where people live may lead to wider questions about what they live close to and how they value access to different parts of their neighbourhood. While young children might focus on their own homes or a nearby street, older children might examine housing types over a wider area, using a range of fieldwork skills to map, draw, measure, survey and respond to issues of design, planning, function and preference.

Finding out why people move homes may start from children's personal experiences and then broaden to consider how, where, when and why people in other places find somewhere else to live. At the local level, moving house can be explored through investigating how houses are bought and sold and people's responses to moving from one place to another. At a wider scale, the decision or necessity to move for different reasons can be seen as part of human history.

Key questions about homes and housing might include:
• Where do they normally live?
• Where else might they sometimes live or visit?
• Who else lives in these places?
• What do these homes look like?
• How long have they lived in their present home?
• Where else have they or their family lived?
• Where are their nearest neighbours?

• How far is their home from school?
• What, if anything, might they change about where they live?
• How do they feel about any changes taking place near their home?

Family structures, household units and homes need flexible interpretation to accommodate children's different backgrounds and avoid anyone feeling left out. Recognising that houses are only one of several places where people may live, both in their own country and elsewhere, helps to set different types of homes into context. Realising that some people may not have a home or a permanent place to live in is part of appreciating different experiences and valuing what it means to have a sense of belonging.

Settlements

Patterns of settlement are a distinctive feature of landscapes throughout the world. Since early attempts at

farming, people's ability to stay in one place with reasonably reliable access to food, water and other supplies has gradually become the dominant lifestyle for the majority of the world's population. Only a small percentage of people, with increasing difficulties, follow a traditional lifestyle which involves regular changes in where they live. Far more of the world's unsettled peoples (which children may hear about in the media and through charity appeals) are now on the move through necessity rather than by choice.

Settled lives rapidly bring change to both people's lifestyles and places. Over time, these changes give distinctive form to settlements, as people's relationship with the environment and those living around them alters. The shift from land-related activities to non-land related activities means that people begin to develop different specialisms which may be exchanged, bartered or sold between each other. People find new ways to display their wealth and power to each other in permanent structures and division of space. Changing actions, ideas and values affect people's behaviour to each other and the land. Such processes give rise to the settlement and landscape patterns children see today. As geographical detectives, they can investigate old and new settlements and perhaps question how places might develop in the future.

Settlements result from many decisions and actions taken over time. Sometimes the reasons for particular choices made by initial settlers

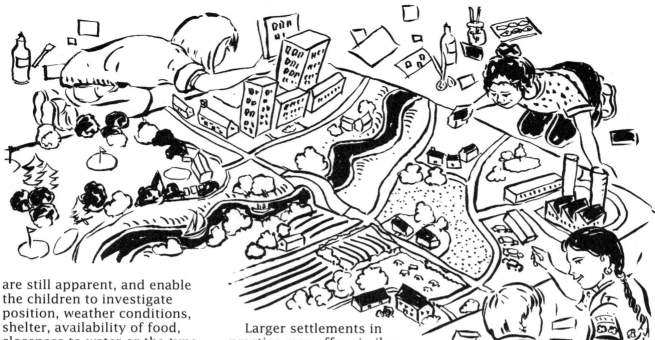

are still apparent, and enable the children to investigate position, weather conditions, shelter, availability of food, closeness to water or the type of rock, soil and minerals in the area. Sometimes original reasons for settlement may be lost under years of subsequent change, and clues about the age, function and character of past lifestyles emerge only through careful fieldwork, map use, talking with people and other forms of investigation.

All settlements offer a wealth of learning possibilities, but site work in a small settlement enables children to gain a sense of a place's identity, its distinctive features and lay-out. A rural settlement has clear physical boundaries. These can be seen both on a map and in reality. Road networks and areas of public and private community life are more definable, and data gathering is generally more manageable. Children can seek, record and interpret evidence of activities and lifestyles at a scale which does not become confusing in its diversity. Problem-solving or issue-based work may be more practical too, around a clearly-defined locally important public concern.

Larger settlements in practice may offer similar potential, once attention focuses on a small locality within the wider whole. Since expanding towns and cities often absorb pre-existing, free-standing smaller settlements, many areas may have an individuality which emerges when children begin to investigate a particular urban area or community close to their school. At primary level, any study of settlement, whatever its size or wherever it is, should involve making discoveries through approaches which help to give a sense of place. Basic questions may be expressed in different ways, but essentially they are transferable to any locality in any geographical setting.

Key questions about settlement might include:
• Where is it?
• What makes it distinctive?
• Who lives there and what is their lifestyle like?
• What activities take place?
• How does it compare with other places and communities?
• How does it connect with other places?

• How and why is it changing?
• How do people respond to any changes which occur?

Other themes

Other examples of popular human geography themes at primary level are explored elsewhere in this book. These activities should suggest, however, that any work on human geography should give children an understanding about aspects of people's interactions with each other and the world around them. Investigations should encourage different ways of working and use varied sources of information. Children should meet different perspectives and lifestyles, and learn to make individual responses which combine sensitive awareness and informed judgement. The following activities are designed with these learning outcomes in mind.

ACTIVITIES

1. People on the move

Objective
To explore patterns of movement by people.

Age range
Seven to eleven.

Group size
Small groups or whole class.

What you need
Enlarged map extracts or pre-drawn street plans, local map, graph paper, writing materials, clip-boards, stop-watch.

What to do
Introduce the theme of transport by asking the children how they normally come to school. Discuss their responses and check if there are variations according to the weather, season or other reasons. This information might be entered into a database or the children might represent individual travel patterns on a graph.

Using enlarged street plans or pre-drawn maps ask the children to identify their route to school, either as a straight line marked with time, or an accurate route from their home to the school gates. You could get them to practise giving directions by asking them to imagine that they are inviting someone home for the first time, and that they are to write a clear set of instructions which will help their new friend reach their home in time for tea.

Further activities
• Ask the children to identify journeys that they have made to different places. Encourage them to suggest ways to classify their journeys. They might sort journeys according to frequency, length, means of travel, purpose or whether they went on their own or with other people. Discuss their findings and look for any patterns in their responses.

• It is helpful to compile a journey logbook over five days, so that the children can use their own data to identify where, when, how often and why they make journeys to different places. Using the data, they can individually or as a class draw graphs and make simple sketch maps which indicate the main places visited, or interrogate it using a database.

• Discuss with the children which forms of transport are appropriate to different journeys in the local area and make either a class or individual transport survey. Ask the children to suggest some of the advantages and disadvantages of different types of travel in the local area. A short survey at home might provide data which

Places we have visited

Name	Place
Krishna	India
Geoffrey	USA
Sally	Australia
Josephine	France
Amanda	Germany
Suzi	Canada
Ravi	Thailand
Lucy	Holland
Pet...	Zealand
Ma...	...les
Alan	...land
Sim...	...a

would alert the children to different types of travelling needs in the local community.
• Fieldwork might include a survey of provision for different kinds of transport in the local area. The children could locate the position of bus-stops, car parks, cycle racks or pedestrianised areas in relation to shops, banks and hospitals. You may also wish to include issues of energy and health and safety in your work.
• The children could make a traffic survey which monitors the amount, type and direction of traffic at different times of day, or on different days of the week. Discuss their findings and ask them to suggest why some times might be busier than others. Look at the route on a local map and ask the children where some of the traffic may be going in each direction. Encourage them to suggest links between causes of traffic and places of work.

2. Long-haul travel

Objective
To introduce children to aspects of travel beyond the local area.

Age range
Seven to eleven.

Group size
Individuals or groups.

What you need
Maps, atlases, pictures, reference books, pre-drawn outlines of countries or world maps, pre-drawn travel itineraries (possibly modelled upon holiday brochures), drawing and art materials, clip-boards, paper, computer software, tourist information, travel brochures, posters, sample travel forms.

What to do
Discuss with the children why people travel beyond the local area. Using atlases, ask the children to locate any places they or members of their family have visited beyond the local area. Each child might have a blank outline map (as appropriate) on which they mark places visited by drawing lines and marking in the actual destination point. Different colours might be used to indicate reasons for travel and routes or patterns of movement made by different members of a family.
Alternatively, the children might locate and trace the approximate route of an international journey using an atlas. You might give them pairs of countries which they have to travel between using different forms of transport. Ask them to identify areas of land and sea, and identify means of travel possible between different places. Using globes, play-mats or satellite pictures, basic awareness of longer journeys can be explored with younger children.

Further activities
• Ask the children to design a passport or find out details of currency, flags and simple greetings appropriate to their route (see Chapter 4 where activities linked to the packing of a suitcase and process of making a journey might be extended).
• Using pictures and a pre-written itinerary, get the children to ask questions about places which might be

visited during a long journey and then ask them to research the answers using reference material. Ask them to sequence pictures and put in order the names of places visited. They might estimate the distances between different places and consider where additional stops might be appropriate. Alternatively, they could consider the number and type of clothes to take for a three or five day journey. Ask them how they might choose to use a camera film with twelve or twenty-four photographs. Using reference books to help with aspects of the journey, they might determine the number and subject of photographs to take per day.

• Some children might use maps or atlases to help them estimate the lengths of different journeys. Ask them to calculate the length of alternative routes or direct 'as the crow flies' distances to different destinations. Introduce real or imaginary reasons for planning alternative routes, such as landslides, weather conditions, political reasons, disease controls or whatever interests the children.

• Children can design simple board games based on making journeys. They could draw a route and then move counters along it according to the picking up of cards or the throw of dice. Ask the children to present their game designs to a geographical selection panel, as this helps them to focus attention on the journey as well as the game.

• With older children, you can examine real or imagined journeys which are longer, more hazardous and expedition-like in character. Real journeys taken in the past

might be mapped, their itineraries plotted, and travel times and conditions compared with current tourist information. Changes in forms of transport between past and present may be identified.

• A visit to a local travel agency gives insights into how some people help others to travel to different destinations. Using research skills, the children could gather data on weather, routes and costs, and store it on a database as part of running a travel agency in the classroom.

• Transport themes might also wish to consider work experiences of people involved as driver, steward, timetable manager, travel sales staff, tour operator, caterer and so on.

• Local controversy over new transport schemes offers older children scope to examine some of the issues through fieldwork, surveys of local

opinion or newspaper reports and meetings with local planners. Presenting their findings in role at a public enquiry, in a class newspaper or exhibition might channel investigation effectively towards a particular audience. Examples of transport changes might include: airport extensions, new roads, rail service closures, re-scheduling of buses or ferries and pedestrianisation schemes.

3. Supply lines

Objective
To identify how goods move from place to place and form links between school, home and wider areas.

Age range
All ages.

Group size

Whole class, individuals, and small groups.

What you need

Large sheets of paper, recording sheets, writing and art materials, reference materials, atlases, wall maps, outline maps, plastic gloves, contacts might be made with environmental or development agencies.

What to do

Brainstorm the goods and supplies which enter school (foods, maintenance materials, consumables and any unusual deliveries). Ask the children to select one of these items and trace the various stages of its journey to school. They can then plot the (approximate) route on an outline map and draw a time line to indicate the length of the journey. They can label the timeline with details of the route and mode of travel.

Further activities

• Ask the children to survey shopping at home. They can collect labels and clean wrappers over several days, identify the products from different countries, and then sort, classify and link them to maps showing their place of origin. Labels, objects or packages could be mounted as part of a display on 'supply lines'.
• Ask the children to suggest how different goods reach the shop shelves or the kitchen cupboard. Ask them to trace the journey of particular goods coming to school or home in a cartoon strip, story or improvisation. Where necessary, get them to research the different stages of the journey and ask large retailers about the international transport of produce between countries. Encourage the children to identify produce which might travel by air and sea.
• Discuss with the children how countries may also supply goods elsewhere, so that other places are not seen only as sources of supplies to their own country. Using a wall map, locate patterns of connection and interdependence.
• Discuss with the children how some materials leave the school site in official ways. Undertake a site survey to identify and plot the routes of pipelines, drains, rubbish bins and removal of waste. Ask the children to locate on a map local landfill sites or incinerators and discuss their role in keeping the local environment clean and controlling pollution.
• Using pictures or descriptions, ask the children to contrast local waste disposal conditions with experiences elsewhere. Discuss waste disposal and the movement of materials in contrasting places. Using news reports and pictures, discuss the problems of transporting oil by sea. Encourage the children to consider risks caused by dumps and landfills. Discuss with them how some children are involved in collecting and scavenging refuse in poor countries.
• Younger children might become archaeologists and investigate how classroom rubbish offers clues about their own lives and actions. A home survey of waste disposal can link lifestyle to issues of recycling. Starting from home or school, young children might also consider how waste is transported for disposal.

Journey of a letter
1. Letter is posted
2. Letter collection
3. Arrival at central sorting office
4. Sorting into different places
5. ?

4. Keeping in contact

Objective
To think about patterns of communication. To consider what happens when communication systems fail to function properly.

Age range
Seven to eleven.

Group size
Individuals, small groups or whole class.

What you need
Clip-boards, enlarged map extracts, paper, cameras, questionnaire sheets, art and writing materials, large site plan.

What to do
Discuss with the children the different forms of communication within the school. Ask them to investigate these communication links with a survey or interviews. They could record their results on a large site plan and compare different patterns of links in different parts of the school.

Ask the children to compare their school findings with a survey in the local area which includes shops, offices, health centres and garages. Ask them to record how the communication varies between different places of work. The children could compile a simple questionnaire to gain this information.

Further activities
• If possible, you could contact the local postal or telephone services and invite speakers into the classroom. The children could send messages by different types of communication. They could investigate how post reaches different destinations and map its route and means of transport. Discuss variations in the postal service between town and countryside and between different countries. Door-to-door deliveries, letter-boxes and individual postal boxes in different countries may be compared. The children could identify how weather or environmental hazards in different countries disrupts communication systems.

• The children could match the purpose of communication and the type of communication system. They might consider how messages differ in their importance. Ask them to compare the amount of time it might take for a letter, telephone call or facsimile message to reach people in different localities, and then illustrate this on a map.

• Using atlases and information on time zones, the children might suggest when messages might be sent and received in contrasting parts of the world. Link-ups between schools in different places can sometimes cross different time zones.

• Communication systems can be explored in many other ways to combine geographical approaches with other curriculum areas. For instance, a study of newspapers and other forms of media can alert children to the influence of time, distance and accessibility upon the selection and presentation of news stories.

• Messages washed up in bottles can introduce mapwork to trace the route of the bottle and a rescue operation, if appropriate.

• The children can locate on a local map where beacons and fires might have been lit to communicate information in the past. Where historical evidence survives, the links between actual beacons may be mapped. Alternatively, historical situations which involve a message being sent

along a chain of look-outs and beacons might be recreated imaginatively. Passing a message can become a practical exercise in the school grounds using hand signals, flags or verbal instructions. Sending a message can become a classroom activity using plastic containers and a length of string.
• Local fieldwork might enable children to identify all the visible features connected with communication on a map or as part of a photographic survey. They could then investigate the purposes of different communication systems in their local area.

5. All in a day's work

Objective
To recognise different aspects of work in contrasting places.

Age range
Seven to eleven.

Group size
Individuals and small groups.

What you need
Writing materials, pictures of people at work in contrasting situations, job advertisements, writing materials, simple questionnaires.

What to do
Discuss with the children the different types of work in school. Identify the tasks and places involved. Establish that work may be indoors, outside, with other people or alone, at different times of day, and involving different kinds of responsibility and skill. Ask them to link their findings to different parts of a school plan or to a clockface.

Further activities
• Surveys of work in and beyond the home can be done by the children. Their findings can be entered in a database so that patterns of work can be related to other factors, such as type of work, place, age of brothers and sisters and so on.
• The children could visit a local place of work and investigate aspects of the work undertaken by its different employees. Large places such as supermarkets, hospitals, factories or travel centres offer a variety of working situations.
• The children could set up an enterprise activity and tackle different tasks within the shared project, for instance, recycling or making a newspaper. The children could write different job descriptions and apply for the positions either in writing or by interview.
• Fieldwork could explore past places of employment in the local area. The children could research a past industry or way of life. They could write letters of application and

prepare for an interview for a job aboard ship, in a mine, on a farm or in a country house. Job advertisements can be compared in the past and present newspapers in contrasting places.
• Investigating work in contrasting localities can be an effective way of introducing the children to more distant places and lifestyles. They could compare the type of work, person at work, tasks, situation and purchasing power of the wages. This can reveal the variety of work experiences faced by men, women and children all over the world (see Chapter 4 and Chapter 12 for further ideas).

6. Playtime pastimes

Objective
To identify how people use non-work time in different ways.

Age range
Seven to eleven.

Group size
Individuals or groups.

What you need
Writing materials, outline maps, atlases, enlarged map extracts, pictures of leisure activities, rulers, graph paper.

What to do
Discuss with the children different kinds of leisure activity. Using pictures, ask them to sort leisure activities into different categories (indoors/outside, town/country, free/paying, energetic/not energetic, organised/unplanned, with/without other people). They may think of some categories of their own.

Using these categories, ask the children to list their family's leisure activities. Ask them to indicate whether they take part in these activities regularly, sometimes, or very rarely. Discuss the patterns in their responses with the children. Ask them if they think their holidays offer different leisure opportunities.

Ask the children to record on a map different places used by their class for leisure. Ask them which places are most and least visited, and why. Encourage the children to link frequency of visits to distance and cost. Get them to compile a bar graph of their visits to leisure places.

Further activities
• Discuss with the children how leisure may affect places in different ways. Ask them if they can think of ways in which visitors can cause problems at different leisure places. Using pictures, ask the children what might make people less or more likely to visit these localities. Ask them to suggest ways of overcoming environmental problems caused by large numbers of visitors and congestion.
• Consider with the children how leisure activities vary from place to place. Compare people's experiences of leisure in different parts of the world. Using pictures, identify how leisure activities may vary in their use of materials and specialised equipment. Encourage the children to try leisure activities from other parts of the world: they could make any equipment required themselves. You could ask them to compare past and present leisure activities in contrasting places and make a distribution map to show leisure activities around the world.
• Leisure activities can also be investigated during fieldwork (see 'Parks and gardens' Chapter 2, page 22).

7. Having a place of one's own

Objective
To observe housing in the local area and to draw upon their own experiences in understanding the design, purpose and individuality of homes. To understand that some people do not have homes.

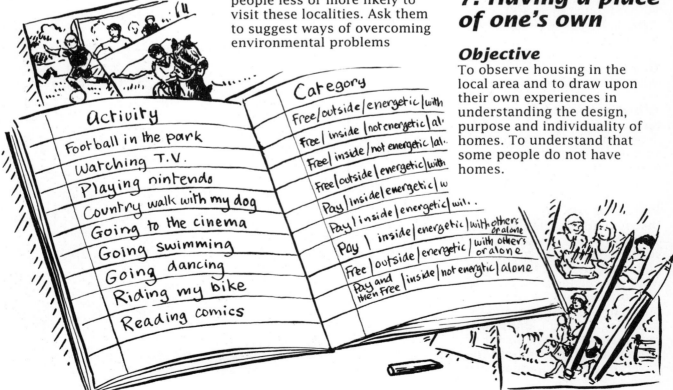

Activity	Category
Football in the park	Free/outside/energetic/with
Watching T.V.	Free/inside/not energetic/al...
Playing nintendo	Free/inside/not energetic/al...
Country walk with my dog	Free/outside/energetic/with
Going to the cinema	Pay/inside/energetic/w
Going swimming	Pay/inside/energetic/wit...
Going dancing	Pay/inside/energetic/with others or alone
Riding my bike	Pay/outside/energetic/with others or alone
Reading comics	Free/outside/energetic/with others or alone
	Pay and then Free/inside/not energetic/alone

Age range
Nine to eleven.

Group size
Individuals or groups.

What you need
Pictures of houses, adhesive, writing and art materials, large sheets of paper, grid square overlays drawn on tracing paper, holiday brochures, estate agents' leaflets, local maps, clip-boards, pre-drawn or enlarged street plans, word processing, database package, reference books.

What to do
Discuss with the children different types of housing. Ask them to identify features of their own homes and encourage them to classify inside and outside details. They might draw or use photographs of their own houses as a basis for labelling different features. Ask them to imagine they could lift off the front of their house and ask them to draw or record words associated with different rooms in the house. Identify vocabulary as appropriate. Ask them to draw a back view too, and label the rooms in a similar way.

Ask the children to mount an assortment of estate-agents'
old photographs (or pictures of local houses) on paper and label as many features as possible. Discuss the different building materials, styles, modifications, dates and examples of how people personalise their homes. Get the children to try to do a scale drawing of one of the houses using a grid overlay onto a larger piece of paper.

Ask the children to compare photographs of housing from different areas using estate agents' pictures, holiday brochures or children's drawings (where school exchanges have been set up). Older children could devise some simple activities for younger children based on pictures of architectural styles in different areas (cut out from holiday brochures).

Further activities
• Arrange a class visit to an estate agent's office to find out how properties are bought and sold. Ask the children to design their own estate agent leaflets for their own home or
other buildings and sites in the local area. They could use computer graphics and a word processing package. Get them to set up an estate agent's office in the classroom and role play the task of buying and selling a house.
• Discuss with the children how and why people move from one place to another. The class could conduct a school survey to see who has experienced buying, selling or moving to another place. They could look at school registers to compare the total numbers of children who enter and leave school during a school year as a result of moves. They could collect photographs or pictures of where different members of the class have lived at different times. They could investigate how people feel at leaving or settling into a house and explore responses through poetry and creative writing.

• Local fieldwork could focus on housing styles. Ask the children to record different types of building materials used in house construction either along a street or at particular stopping places on a walk. They could also record how people give identity to their gardens, house frontages, porches or windows on maps of the local area or a pre-drawn plan of houses along a residential road. They could design ways of personalising their own homes and then discuss how individual wishes may sometimes be constrained by community or neighbourhood interests.

• Discuss with the children the different kinds of accommodation that there are (bedsits, flats, houses). Ask them to think what it might be like to have no home and live on their streets. Discuss some of the reasons why people are homeless. Compare homelessness in different parts of the world.

• Using pictures, ask the children to compare the homes of rich and poor in different localities and countries. Then discuss the photographs and identify similarities and differences. Ask the children to write about living in another country from informative material. Alternatively, ask them to present a case at a housing office for having basic accommodation, improving a modest home or converting a large house into many homes. Ask them to list the points they would use to justify their request.

8. Towns that change shape

Objective
To understand how settlements change through time. To think about the process of how settlements first develop. To think about conflicts caused by settlement development. To remind children that some people in the world traditionally have not lived in permanent places.

Age range
Nine to eleven.

Group size
Individuals or groups.

What you need
Writing paper, pictures of settlements, maps, atlases, large-scale map extracts of the local area, set of briefing cards, reference books, historical maps of the local area, local census information, local street directories.

What to do
Discuss with the children how people have basic physical needs such as shelter, food and liquid. Ask them to make their own list of things they think are basic needs for their everyday lives. Discuss how their list may be divided into 'essential' and 'non-essential' categories and ask them to suggest which of their needs are more important.

Identify how their needs are associated with other places. List the types of buildings and services that are connected to their everyday needs. Using large-scale map extracts, ask the children to locate places in the local area that are associated with the different needs of their everyday life. Identify how these features of everyday living influence the type and number of buildings in a settlement.

Give the children pictures of contrasting settlements. Ask them to describe the pictures and sort them according to size. Discuss any visual clues about what activities take place in settlements of different sizes. Locate the settlements on regional maps. Ask the children to suggest what people might do when their needs cannot be met in a small settlement. Discuss the reasons for journeys elsewhere. Ask the children to compare the appearance of the different settlements. Encourage them to use the visual clues to help them to imagine and describe living, working, travelling, going to school and enjoying themselves in these places. Ask them to compare a day in the life of someone in contrasting settlements. Introduce them to material about life in other settlements when appropriate.

Discuss how settlements develop in different ways. Ask the children why a settlement grows or shrinks in size. Ask them if they know any reasons why their own settlement should grow or shrink in size

or get them to sort ideas using briefing cards. Ask what might happen to their settlement if it grows in size or people move away; for example, what might happen to the services or housing developments?

Discuss the different opinions people might have about the expansion of their settlement, which people might be in favour and which opposed. Ask the children to imagine they are town planners. They have to choose a local site for new housing or industrial development. Ask them to suggest reasons for and against the development of sites inside or on the edge of the existing settlement, using maps. The children could visit and survey the actual site (see Chapter 7).

Ask the children to imagine what it might be like if all their neighbours moved away and the local shops or their own school closed. Where appropriate, use descriptions and photographs of real

examples to help the children imagine what shrunken or deserted settlements might be like. Encourage creative responses in writing, drama, music and art.

Further activities

• Discuss maps showing how the local settlement has changed through time. Using photographs, street directories and census information ask the children to investigate part of the locality. Where possible, invite older visitors to talk about parts of the settlement which have changed and look for visible clues in local streets. Help the children to construct a timeline which shows dates and phases of change and development in the local area. Families often provide photographs and other mementoes which help to relate settlement changes to people's lives and enrich a study of the local area.

• If new housing development occurs in the local area, ask the children to consider the conflict of interests between providing homes and work, and nature conservation or keeping farm land. The children could interview local people and carry out fieldwork on the proposed redevelopment site, prior to the start of construction work. They might also consider why some areas are more suitable than others for housing development.

• Ask the children to imagine that they are to move away from the local area and are going to create a new life for themselves in another place.

Ask them to list what they would take with them and to suggest how they might select a suitable place to go to. Discuss how people might miss certain parts of their old lifestyle and seek to recreate it in their new home and surroundings. Get the children to suggest how the introduction of these things from their past home might alter the appearance of their new surroundings. Ask which places and features they would like to have in their new home (roads, bridges, buildings, open spaces, farms). Discuss the conflicts they might have with other people already living in the place and how these conflicts could be suitably solved. You could then extend the initial

imaginary situation into real contexts, using historical examples of settlement expansion into areas already inhabited by other people.

• Tell the children that there are people in the world who traditionally move around rather than live in one place. Locate some traditional nomadic people on a world map. Contrast aspects of their lives in the past and present. Using pictures, music, stories and reference materials, discuss the characteristics of nomadic lives and encourage the children to think about the advantages and disadvantages of not living permanently in a settlement. Discuss why nomadic ways of life are now under threat in most parts of the world.

Reflections

Human geography invites children to question and interpret many of the patterns of activity and behaviour in the world around them. It involves thinking about familiar aspects of their lives and searching for underlying reasons and meanings. It explores patterns of similarity and difference in contrasting places. Opportunities to encounter diversity and common experience or shared need, offer scope for recognising the strengths and shortcomings which are to be found in different places and lifestyles. Learning to respect the diversity which

occurs in almost any geographical setting is an important element in developing children's awareness.

Children's curiosity, comprehension and level of awareness must determine how and when ideas and issues are developed. More abstract issues may often only be touched upon through discussion or extension activities and perhaps, even then, with only a few children. Where to pitch ideas must depend on a teacher's ability to judge what has meaning, interest and potential for all, some and individual children.

Children's interest in geography often derives

from concern with the familiar or the excitement of the unknown. Opportunities to channel this interest exist in problem-solving activities and issue-based approaches. This chapter and the next identify many themes where real issues and decision-making processes are investigated. Children enjoy meeting and working with outside experts in their own search for information and solutions. While issues which extend to other localities may lack the immediacy of local investigation, there may be potential school visitors with experiences to share to a classroom audience.

CHAPTER 7

Environmental geography

Popular concern for environmental causes is more apparent than ever before. Looking after the planet has become a subject of debate that sends ripples into homes, communities and organisations, from local to global level. As environmental concerns permeate aspects of daily and political life in different ways around the world, primary classrooms resound with children's calls to protect the earth.

Many children are receptive to campaigns, appeals and constant media cover of environmental destruction and degradation. Although some children remain indifferent, many others have become self-appointed watchdogs of domestic and community environmental behaviour. Fostering environmental awareness among the young requires bringing together informed understanding and sensitivity.

Global concerns should not obscure local issues and possibilities for personal action. Threatened ecosystems and endangered species elsewhere should not mean local wildlife and habitats are overlooked.

Conservation means people and places as well as plants and animals. Protecting the environment means thinking about lifestyles and challenging assumptions too. Children need to recognise the links between human, physical and environmental processes, as well as identify and begin to overcome contradictions in their own lifestyles. Helping them to approach complex and often emotive issues with sensitivity and informed judgement, brings a more critical basis for personal convictions and commitment.

BACKGROUND

Environmental awareness has long been the concern of environmental education with its well-established strands of learning *about, through* and *for* the environment and its commitment to cross-curricular approaches. Finding a place for these concerns within the primary curriculum is increasingly important as the world's environmental problems grow.

Environmental concerns involve children in many areas of knowledge, ways of working and introduce them to varied points of view. Fostering awareness and a sense of environmental and social responsibility is central to children's overall development and must therefore be integral to the whole school curriculum. Recognising how people and environment interact is also vital to understanding processes of geographical change.

An environmental approach

Environmental matters lie at the heart of geographical investigation. Geography concerns interaction between the earth and its people, and explores how these relationships find visible expression in the landscape as well as issues, ideas, interpretations and actions. Geographical knowledge and understanding depend on varied working methods and require children to present their findings in different ways.

A geographical approach looks for patterns which link places, peoples and processes together and locates environmental concerns within distinctive settings. Maps or photographs provide both a source and a base for information. Varied sources are used to seek answers to geographical questions and analysis might draw upon skills and ideas from other curriculum areas. Investigations include fieldwork wherever possible and seek local connections when looking at environmental issues related to other places.

Critical viewing brings media cover of environmental issues into the classroom.

CITIES   RIVERS
CARS   OIL

POLLUTION IN BRITAIN IN THE 1990s

CAR EXHAUST HIGHER THAN...

Models and experiments simulate and compare environmental conditions. Drama and role play explore ideas, actions and different responses to environmental predicaments. Contacts with professionals and outside agencies alert children to decision-making processes and contrasting perspectives.

Geographical investigations set environmental preferences, predicaments and priorities within the diversity of lifestyle and need throughout the world. Environmental concerns and alternative options are met at different scales of activity and intensity in and beyond local levels. Wherever possible, informed understanding should be related to practical action and personal involvement.

Places under pressure

Environmental problems occur at a variety of scales. Although media attention may focus upon particular regions, most places are threatened by pressures of some kind. Children should be aware of the variety of environmental pressures and identify that

similar processes may underlie very different environmental problems.

Pressures and problems associated with recent changes in the countryside affect the environment in many ways. Children might investigate the changes in landscape, livelihood and lifestyle which occur where they live. Observable changes in rural areas might include building development, road construction, farm practice, forestry, power stations, leisure activities, holiday homes and tourism. Less visible changes might include crop spraying, pollution and wildlife conservation. Fieldwork might be supplemented by practical activities including tree-planting, developing wildlife habitats, path improvement or making suggestions for the sign of way-markers, trails, interpretation or picnicking facilities for countryside visitors.

In urban areas, places under pressure might range from a single building to a whole district of a town or city. Children should focus on a

small area for detailed site-work and investigation. Conversion of old buildings, new homes, developing play or sitting areas, making traffic-free zones, tackling traffic and litter problems, or upgrading public open space, are some of the many environmental themes to explore in towns. Investigations should involve consultation with planners and people who live and work in the area. Finding opportunities where children can be involved in real planning issues or improvement projects can lead to rewarding urban environmental work with primary children.

At a global level, many kinds of urban and rural environment face different types of pressures. The availability of information and teaching resources suitable for primary children will affect the extent of practical work, but by using materials produced by different government, development and environmental agencies, many issues can be effectively

Resources and the environment

developed as part of a wider thematic approach or focus on a particular locality. More distant urban environmental concerns likely to attract interest at primary level include housing, transport and water, although other local issues prompt comparisons with elsewhere. Rural environmental issues may also include farming, the impact of tourism upon wildlife and landscape, deforestation, desertification, drought and global warming.

Activities and approaches should start from children's experiences, learning needs and perspectives. The effects of environmental pressures upon places and people at any scale should include considering the implications for children. Recognising how environmental change may affect themselves or children elsewhere gives meaning to issue-based work at local or wider levels.

Environmental geography should foster a sense of personal responsibility and active involvement in their own locality. Environmental improvements might begin with making places better for the young. A focus on playspace under threat, for instance, readily widens into development pressures upon land and issues of jobs, homes and conservation. Many local issues illustrate global environmental processes too. Local tree clearance might be linked to rainforest destruction. Seasonal water restrictions, pipe laying or a survey of daily activities might prompt them into considering how water shortage affects the lives of children elsewhere. Familiar experiences and observable processes thus effectively carry children's environmental concerns across geographical distance.

Children should learn that people use, value and respond to their surroundings in different ways. Geography introduces children to how people attach importance and value to different aspects of the world around them and identify different types of resources.

Many of the world's major environmental issues concern resources. Fulfilling people's needs and expectations brings the world's resources under increasing pressure, and children must recognise that these issues occur at a variety of levels. Investigations enable children to encounter some of the resource conflicts that happen in their own locality and community and elsewhere. First-hand observations help to identify how resources satisfy people's wants and needs in different ways. Direct experiences offer children a basis for understanding that places and peoples around the world are threatened by various patterns and processes of resource abuse, misuse and unequal use.

Children should identify that they depend upon a variety of resources. They can list different types of resources, although classifying resources is not always straightforward. Older children might examine how they make use of environmental resources and where physical materials come from. They can use maps to trace their own connections with other places, where landscapes, lives and livelihoods are influenced by the needs and expectations of people elsewhere. Recognising patterns of interdependence from local to global level helps children to value different contributions to their own lives and to foster positive understanding about other people and places.

Patterns of resource extraction and use affect lives and landscapes in contrasting ways. Looking at the implications of resource use might involve fieldwork, questionnaires, surveys or site appraisals on aspects of environmental change. Landscape change brought about by redevelopment, mines, quarries and leisure pursuits or forestry, farming and transport offers much scope for mapping, fieldwork and other surveys. Searching for solutions which avoid simplistic reasoning, requires children to encounter different viewpoints, gather data and interpret with sensitivity.

Environmental issues in other localities also require sensitive awareness and balanced interpretation. Studies of resource depletion must sift facts from fiction and safeguard against sensationalism and stereotyping either victims or villains. Issues which are global in significance may also occur locally. Any environment-based work might thus start from a distant or local perspective and ideally make appropriate connections in between.

Resource depletion issues might include deforestation, energy, soil erosion, water and the degradation of seas and polar regions.

Environmental protection

Recognising the importance of protecting the environment stems from children becoming aware of how certain activities and attitudes may spoil places for plants, animals and other people. Environmental awareness and responsibility develops from encouraging children to look after their surroundings and to behave appropriately in town, country and at school. Young children must learn that they each have an important role in safeguarding their surroundings so that others may enjoy them too. Behaving

responsibly towards the world around them helps children to recognise that other people in different ways may be involved in caring for places too.

Children should encounter contrasting types of protected places at different scales. They should think about how some places acquire special value and gain protection, while others are overlooked and neglected. Their own area may have sites which have significance in different ways for local children and adults. They might consider why particular landscapes and environments come under threat and how their capacity to withstand change differs. They should recognise that people's influence to bring about or resist change also varies.

Such concerns may be as applicable to a patch of waste land in a town or a wilderness. The character and purpose of parks, nature reserves, and other protected sites of local, regional, national and international significance should be identified through maps and pictures, eye-witness accounts, stories and ideally direct experience. Where access to protected sites is restricted, perhaps children might become involved in up-grading and safe-guarding part of their own doorstep environment.

Environment preferences

Environmental awareness requires children to go beyond finding out about their surroundings. Questioning *how* people make sense of what they see, *where* they like to be and *why* people like or notice different features in and around where they live, introduces children to more subjective responses to the environment.

Understanding that places as well as people change through time is important in environmental geography. Seeking clues about physical changes which have occurred in the local area, or individual buildings, introduces young children to different kinds of change – large/small, fast/slow, intended/unintended, and leads on to thinking whether changes can improve or spoil places and buildings. Children can record additions, removals or conversions for their school or local street on a time-line or outline school plan.

Considering past action leads to thinking how places might be affected by future change. Children can compare different ways of improving a particular place. The variety of responses, conflicting interests, constraints and possibilities which affect the potential for change could involve site work, consultation with different people, meeting outside experts and devising plans for real or imaginary changes in or close to their school.

Children gain insight into environmental matters through working on a model, role-play or other imaginary context. Still better, the opportunity to bring about changes in a practical situation, through improving part of their school site, making a wildlife garden for a local nursery or even taking over a corner of waste land can give environmental action lasting significance for children.

ACTIVITIES

1. Likes and dislikes

Objective
To identify how people interpret their surroundings in different ways.

Age range
Seven to eleven.

Group size
Individuals or small groups.

What you need
Large sheets of paper, writing materials, prepared questionnaires, rulers, graph paper or a database program.

What to do
Compile a list of types of places or named places which the children like or dislike. Compile a word bank of words, phrases and comments which express their responses to particular places or simply describe them. Compare responses within the class and discuss why preferences for particular places might vary.

Further activities
Ask the children to carry out a survey of likes and dislikes at home or in another class. If they design a questionnaire, they might include such questions as:
• What are your favourite kinds of places?
• Suggest phrases which remind you of these places.
• What kinds of places do you dislike?

• Suggest some words or phrases which indicate why you dislike these places...
Encourage the children to compare their findings in small groups or as a class. They need to gather the responses and classify them according to places people like and dislike. Discuss with the children any patterns evident in the responses and ask them to see if answers vary according to age or gender. Responses could be sorted numerically and represented as bar graphs or pie-charts. Alternatively, the children might compile a written report on their findings.

2. Pleasing prospects

Objective
To encourage children to observe environmental evidence closely. To consider the effects of change.

Age range
All ages.

Group size
Individuals or small groups.

What you need
Pictures which show a variety of landscapes, writing materials, word processing package.

What to do
Introduce the children to pictures and postcards of contrasting places. Discuss the colours, shapes, patterns, sounds, smells and different features shown or suggested by the views. Distribute the pictures and ask the children to list details of colour, shape and pattern and any sounds, smells or tastes suggested by

each picture. Encourage them to think how they might feel about or respond to each scene. Compare the responses. Some children may like to write about a particular picture.

Ask the children to imagine that they could change one thing in their picture. They should identify what that change might be and how it might affect the scene and their feelings towards the scene. This might form the basis for discussion, or for written work on places where change is likely or has occurred.

Further activities

The children could use pictures or postcards to test whether particular landscape features (water, forest, sea, clouds, buildings) influence how people respond to particular scenes. Postcard views might test townscape preferences in a similar way. Using a set of five landscape views, they might question people about their preferences and note down their responses. Their survey could include such questions as:
• Do you find this scene unattractive/quite attractive/very attractive?
• What do you like most about this scene?
• What do you like least about this scene?
• Would you like to visit this place? Not at all/not really/quite a lot/very much.

The survey findings can be sorted numerically, so that the children can identify people's preferences for different kinds of place. Visits to other classrooms should be undertaken in pairs and with prior warning. The children might compare the responses of adults and other children.

3. Place poems

Objective
To observe and make a written subjective response to a particular place.

Age range
Seven to eleven.

Group size
Individuals or small groups.

What you need
Clip-boards, writing materials, camera, portable recording equipment, word processing package.

What to do
Take the children to a vantage point within the school grounds, or any other safe place where they can observe their surroundings safely. You can either base the children at a particular point or take them on a short walk. Brainstorm on words associated with the place or ask them to think about and note down any words, phrases and ideas suggested by the general character of the place.

Encourage the children to note colours, movements, sounds, smells and textures. In each case, remind them to note permanent details and then to look for aspects which might change at different times of the day, season or even as they watch and write, such as sunlight, shadows, people passing by and so on. Check with the children that they have noted everything that makes the place distinctive and unmistakable from somewhere else. Back in the classroom they should each write their 'place poem' based on this work.

Further activities
• The children could take photographs of places to go with their 'place poems'. Display the pictures and text together. They could produce an illustrated anthology of 'place poems' to share with another class or sell as an enterprise project to family and friends.

• Get the children to make sound recordings of places using portable cassette recorders. Back in the classroom, get them to try to create environmental poems which combine recorded sounds, recreated sound effects and verbal responses by experimenting with instruments and their tape recordings.

4. Wordscapes

Objective
To evaluate the quality of the surroundings and environmental perception.

Age range
Nine to eleven.

Group size
Individuals, pairs or groups.

What you need
Clip-boards, writing materials, large map extract, pictures, maps or an atlas.

What to do
Plan a short circular walk which takes the children into contrasting places beyond the school site. Before leaving the classroom, identify on the map extract the route and stopping places, and organise the children into small groups. Tell the children that they should describe each stopping place, as accurately as they can, by using words and phrases to record their impressions and sensory responses. Encourage them to use words imaginatively as they work at the different sites. Walk the route and ask the children to complete their list for each site. Afterwards, compare the children's responses and ask them to write more fully about the different stopping places. Alternatively, ask the children to devise signs or symbols for aspects of each site which they can add to the map extract.

This activity could be used to introduce work upon environmental improvement, since it encourages observation and structured recording which might prompt discussion about remedial action in different places.

Further activities
• The children's responses could be entered into a database and compared with other observations made at different seasons or times at the same stopping places. They might also note the influence of weather upon their surroundings.
• Working indoors from sets of five pictures, children can use the word lists in a similar way and discuss any patterns in their responses. Pictures might be located using an atlas.

5. Theme walks

Objective
To map aspects of the local environment (such as visual features, environmental quality, litter, pollution and community needs).

Age range
All ages.

Group size
Whole class, pairs or small groups.

What you need
Photocopied large-scale map extracts, drawing and art materials, Plasticine, clip-boards, notebooks, cassette recorders or cameras, hand-lens (for detailed work), collecting containers.

What to do
Discuss with the children what themes would be suitable to

explore on a walk in the local area. Older children might carry out an initial survey to select an appropriate theme. Suitable themes could be: patterns, colours, design features, textures, surfaces, outlines, skylines, shapes, sound, uses of land and buildings, wear and tear, old and new, access and so on.

Ask the children how they might record their observations. Get them to look at evidence on their map extracts and identify an agreed code of symbols for recording the information. Divide the children into pairs before leaving the classroom.

Position the children in the study area to record, gather material and make observations. Ensure that they name all their data with its location before leaving the site and note the photo-stops (if working with cameras). A video version of this work is also possible (see Chapter 9).

In the classroom, ask the children to transfer information on their selected theme to a clean map extract. Once they have established a site map, ask them to devise a trail so that others might follow their theme. They need to consider how to give clear directions and how they might present their trail in different ways. For younger children, the task of putting their findings in sequence is usually sufficient. For older children trails are usually more interesting to devise than follow, so they might develop their work with another audience in mind, such as younger children or visitors. Their audience will influence decisions on how to present information.

A display including the base map or site plan and associated information and labels might conclude the work. Alternatively, a scavenger route with clues might enable younger children to follow the trail, marking in their discoveries at particular places. Examples of published town trail leaflets might offer ideas about the design of a visitor trail and the children could use software programs to devise theirs.

Further activity
Ask the children to imagine that they are a local tourist officer. They are to design a visitor's guide or thematic town trail leaflet. They need to use street plans and other reference materials to devise a self-guiding trail and text suitable for visitors. They might need to consider such issues as:
• the shortest possible walking circuit of tourist sites;
• a cycle route following the one-way system;
• accommodation for a disabled or elderly visitor within easy reach of key tourist features;
• areas for car parking or congested streets to avoid.

6. Planning in green and grey

Objective
To apply mapping skills in realistic situations.

Age range
Nine to eleven.

Group size
Pairs or small groups.

What you need
Large photocopies or a simplified map extract of the local area, art and writing materials, access to local planners, copies of local newspapers, copies of real planning application forms (simpler versions should be developed for use with younger children).

What to do
Introduce children to the work of town planners. Identify how they make decisions which influence the appearance and activities of any area. Show the children local examples of planning activities. Discuss some of the planning decisions which influenced the development of the school.

Brainstorm with the children on issues which planners might have to consider in choosing sites such as a school, adventure playground, leisure centre and so on. Ask the children to suggest how local people might react to different planning proposals. Discuss with the children why conflicting interests develop over planning proposals. Local newspapers often provide planning issues which illustrate these processes effectively.

Ask the children to imagine that they are local planners.

Distribute large-scale map extracts and ask them to decide where to locate a new purpose-built tourist information and travel centre. They should choose their site carefully. Remind them that local people may hold contrasting views on the promotion of tourism, so they must consider how to present proposals effectively.

Further activities
• Ask the children to imagine that they represent development companies that wish to undertake certain projects. Discuss with the children why some sites might be more suitable than others for different kinds of development. Compile a class list of issues to consider when choosing a site. The list might include: traffic, noise, appearance, parking, access and so on. With the help of large-scale maps, the children should decide in groups which site might be suitable for different planning proposals. Ask each group to present its case for development and justify its choice of site to the rest of the class, who collectively might be the town council. Development requests might include: a large superstore, a disco, a leisure centre, sheltered housing for the elderly and a bus station.
• This activity could be extended as a planning role-play in which each development company submits a written and spoken proposal at a planning enquiry. Each proposal must be submitted in advance, so that another group of children can devise a case ' for' or 'against' the application. The rest of the class must decide on the basis of presented evidence and views, and then vote to reject or accept (outright or with modification) the proposals. An adult should chair the planning enquiry.
• The class could plan a new settlement. Each development company could then take responsibility for devising one plot on a large pre-drawn plan which could become the base for a model town with homes, shops, public buildings, services and amenity areas. Planning applications could be submitted at a planning

AERIAL PHOTOGRAPH

MUSEUM GUIDE

enquiry. Once the plans gain acceptance, they could be designed as models to fit within each plot. Such a project could take half-a-term to complete in detail.

7. Town planning teasers

Objective
To think about processes of environmental change in the local area.

Age group
Nine to eleven.

Group size
Individuals or small groups.

What you need
Photocopies of large-scale map extracts or pre-drawn enlarged street plans of the immediate vicinity of the school, writing materials.

What to do
Ask the children to imagine that they are town planners and are responsible for a number of changes in the local area. An introductory discussion may help the children to identify some of the issues. Remind them to use their map extracts to help them find practical solutions. Ask them to consider:
• a one-way system to control traffic movement through the central area;
• a temporary diversion to avoid the central area, where a procession, fair or carnival will take place over a holiday weekend;
• a method which a marketing company (with a team of five helpers working equally hard) could use to distribute leaflets throughout part of the settlement as quickly as possible;
• a price tariff for a newly-formed dial-a-dinner service (or equivalent) to places within equal delivery time in different parts of the settlement;
• a new network of post-boxes or level-crossings for one part of the town; the most suitable places for the minimal effective number of collections or crossing points must be marked on a map.

Ask the children to present their solutions to the rest of the class or to write a short report for the local newspaper, using a word processing package (see Chapter 10).

8. Photo-surveys

Objective
To collect visual evidence about aspects of their surroundings.

Age range
Seven to eleven.

Group size
Small groups.

What you need
Camera, film, clip-boards, writing materials.

What to do
Plan a short circular walk, along which the children will be able to find different kinds of visual evidence about the local area. Identify photo-stops in advance or ask them to select viewpoints for a photo-survey. They might concentrate on signs, wires and cables, water, roads, open spaces and so forth. Alternatively, ask them to look for intentional and unintentional patterns beside, below, above and around them. Once they have made their photo-survey, they should write about what their photographs show and comment on these aspects of their surroundings.

Further activities
Ask the children to be environmental detectives. Using a camera they should gather visual evidence of litter or environmental eyesores during a local walk. They

might investigate how remedial action could be taken and talk with local people or planners. They might use their photographs as part of a campaign for change. Their photographs might become a resource for comparisons if future changes occur.

9. Changing views

Objective
To examine what happens when scenes are changed by introducing something different.

Age range
Seven to eleven.

Group size
Individuals or small groups.

What you need
Pictures of scenes in urban or rural areas (including those from photographs, colour magazines and brochures), art and writing materials, adhesive, Blu-Tack, scissors, masking tape, tracing paper, acetate sheets, pens, clip-boards, reprints of old photographs.

What to do
Discuss with the children the appearance of different landscape or street scenes using pictures. Ask them to identify different features in the views. Get them to imagine the scene is changed in some way and discuss the effects. For instance, discuss how new buildings can alter the appearance of older ones or an existing street or affect a previously unbuilt area. Ask the children to consider how scenes are changed by the removal or addition of natural or unnatural features. Ask them to experiment using cut-outs on different backgrounds.

Comments on the effects of making changes can be written and displayed with the changed views.

Further activities
• Ask the children to make a picture montage of either a real or imaginary landscape, using features cut from different sources. Discuss the effect of alternative features which might enhance or spoil the scene. Ask them to experiment using Blu-Tack to fix different features on their background. Encourage them to write about the effects of different changes.
• Ask the children to draw different surroundings for photographed features. They might place their photograph on a large sheet of paper and extend it into a wider view,

using art materials, acetate sheets or tracing paper, so that different settings can be superimposed on the photographic detail.

• Where this activity forms part of fieldwork, ask the children to experiment with changes to simple field sketches drawn on a previous occasion. They might use photographs of particular features as starting points for changing views and settings.

• Introduce the children to past and present views of a familiar place. Reprints of old photographs are ideal for this activity and you could involve the children in taking photographs from the same viewpoint. Ask them to compare the features in the different views and to record any changes. Ask them to identify any features which have remained unchanged. Get them to classify the types of change they can spot in the photographs. Discuss with the children the effects of change in their photographs. Aspects of recent change might be within memory and worth linking with interviews in the local community. You could ask the children to write about the photographs.

10. Pressure points

Objective
To consider the effects of change in other localities.

Age range
Seven to eleven.

Group size
Individuals or small groups.

What you need
A variety of pictures showing urban or rural scenes in unfamiliar localities, reference books, writing materials.

What to do
Hand out pictures of less familiar places and ask the children to identify the main characteristics in the scene. Ask them to brainstorm or note as many details as they can. Ask them to suggest three changes which might improve the scene in each photograph. If there are people in the photograph, encourage them to suggest what changes each person might like to see. Discuss and compare the children's responses. As a class, consider what influences change. Wherever possible, try to offer the children examples which show both positive and negative changes.

Further activities
Ask the children to imagine that the scene in a photograph is under threat and official plans to build, flood, develop or otherwise change it are currently being made. Using evidence in the photograph, and other information, work out a case 'for' or 'against' the site's protection.

CHAPTER 8

Starting from stories

Stories are everywhere! Stories have been at the centre of language ever since words have been able to transmit basic ideas and values from one generation to the next. How we see, experience and make sense of the world is influenced by an endless stream of narrative. Whether printed, spoken or broadcast, stories which support, confirm or challenge our perceptions of the world constantly surround us. In our search for meaning and understanding, we become both providers and consumers of stories from an early age.

This chapter explores how reading, hearing, telling and making stories contribute to primary geography. The very origins of geography derive from the Greek words meaning 'earth' and 'to write', and the following suggestions are relevant to sharing and creating stories in varied ways with different age groups. Children can practise many different skills as they read, hear, depict, dance or act out written responses to the places, characters and situations encountered in different settings.

Stories belong to an older oral tradition in which their purpose was always two-fold, not only to teach but also to entertain. Starting from stories must not lose the magic and power of the imagination in searching for geographical potential. Indeed, learning to listen and enjoy may reveal that many stories have more than one lesson to teach. Stories with meanings that grow and change at different times may offer a lasting understanding that should not be cast lightly aside.

Stories and worlds of experience

Stories fulfil many social, emotional, psychological and intellectual needs. Stories within geography seem to form a bridge between the physical and human worlds. Physical and natural elements have powers and characteristics independent of any human activity and yet we depend on them. Children need to develop an understanding of this world, to be able to locate themselves within it and to appreciate their relationship and responsibility towards it. Much of this is at the core of geography for younger children, and underpins activities which enable them to investigate and respond to the variety within both familiar and less familiar environments.

There is another world, however, that exists only because the individual child exists. It is a highly individual world built of feeling, sensations and personal meanings, shaped by associations and imagination. If mapped, it would comprise private spaces and places built out of experience and perception. These personal geographies and mental maps should feature within children's developing locational frameworks. The price of finding oneself in the real-world must not be at the cost of losing an intimate meaningful relationship with an inner world.

Stories help to connect inner and outer worlds. Words and images bring meaning and foster children's appreciation for the world in which they live. The narrative process in legend, folk-tale, or other story form helps to structure, synthesise or reveal aspects of human and natural existence. It may inform, comment upon or seek to explain. It may redefine or reinforce cultural traditions and beliefs. It may challenge or consolidate perspectives through addressing the familiar or exploring the unknown. Whether old or modern, individual or inherited, concerned with fact or fantasy, stories usually spring from roots in something recognisable which, however slight, provides a basis for constructing new meaning.

A *place for stories*

Opportunities to build geographical understanding through stories occur in various ways. News bulletins, or stories from different cultures during assemblies, might prompt enquiries into themes (such as lifestyle, environmental attitudes and wider concerns about human existence or the natural world). Finding ways to respond geographically to these inherently geographical stories is sometimes lost under the welter of exciting cross-curricular activities which may develop. It is therefore important to recognise how follow-up activities are directing children's responses.

Stories provide an exciting start to research, analysis and interpretation in a geographical study. Whether news reports, eye-witness accounts or fiction, reading aloud or re-telling a story can kindle interest and imaginative thinking. Selecting a story which will sustain its inherent quality, as well as fire children's enthusiasm for geographical investigation over several weeks, requires careful planning. The story must not be overworked and its suitability for specific geography-related activities must be gauged. Using the geographical opportunities should cease before either the children begin to groan or the story starts to creak!

Story-time can be a valuable opportunity for fostering geographical thinking. Sometimes, the choice of story may stem directly from a particular piece of work involving the whole class and, in a sense, extend the children's thinking about related issues. Where the children are focused on another area of the curriculum, reading a story to the class with a geographical flavour can consolidate earlier learning, and keep some geographical awareness at least in the back of children's minds!

Ideally, stories should be used with other geographical sources to help children visualise different places and lifestyles. Sometimes personal accounts, legends, fables, news items, extracts from longer stories or diaries, may be better seen as a source of evidence to set alongside fieldwork or other classroom activities (such as mapping, using artefacts or data handling package), rather than as a subject matter for story-time.

Stories with a strong geographical slant may provide a vehicle for other areas of the curriculum. For example, when attention is focused on reading, writing and number work, a story-line with clear concerns about a distinctive place can bring freshness to more routine concerns about area, punctuation or grammar!

Choosing stories

Many children's stories are set within places and periods (either real or imaginary) and involve characters with which children can readily identify, empathise or react to. The

spatial or temporal settings, characters and situations in many stories offer opportunities for developing different aspects of geographical understanding.

Stories may be useful if they have a strong sense of place, or if they show how places and points of view change through time. Geographical vocabulary may help to set the scene, describe activities or people-place relations. Words and pictures may provide a basis for comparison between the direct experience of here and now, and the imagined reality of there and then. Some stories powerfully evoke a sense of a locality in or beyond the home area, and offer insights into place, lifestyle and circumstances.

There may be spatial aspects which can be simply modelled, mapped or compared with a more familiar setting, living arrangements, present attitude or form of behaviour. Distinctive landscapes or settlements may

have clearly defined layouts through which the characters or objects move and interact. A journey or route at any scale may enable mapwork, route-planning or, for older children, timetabling activities.

Specific geographical ideas might arise in stories and prompt discussion or extension activities using other information sources. Details of landscape, landform and lifestyle may illustrate aspects of geographical explanation and change.

Sometimes stories explore geographical concerns from a perspective rooted in children's experience and interests. Stories can thus give children an entry point into a place and way of life quite different from anything they have met before, and yet draw upon some area of familiar or personal knowledge. Meeting the worlds of school, play, home, work, television and holidays in stories gives important formal recognition and value to everyday experiences and illustrates that geographical interests, like stories, are everywhere!

Working with stories

Stories help to introduce young children to people, places and ideas: from these fictional or indirect encounters it should be possible through contact with actual people, photographs, artefacts and other sources of evidence to develop additional understanding of place and lifestyle. Stories can thus trigger children's geographical imagination for explorations of actuality which may use maps, plans, databases, interviews, pictures, sound recordings, artefacts and field-work to give meaning to fictional form.

When stories are read from illustrated texts, broadcast on television or shown in picture or cartoon form, children build up mental pictures which teachers can supplement or (as in the case of comics) perhaps challenge by offering alternative images. Where available materials require teachers to become storytellers of unillustrated texts, children are totally reliant upon imagination and their mental pictures depend upon the power of the words to covey meaning. As visual (rather than oral communication) now dominates in much of the world, the telling of stories may be daunting, as traditional skills of telling and listening can no longer be taken for granted.

Storytelling varies from culture to culture, but its popularity and vitality within oral tradition relies upon the shared enjoyment of creating words and imagined worlds together. Storyteller and listener both play an active role. Telling a story requires knowing it well first, and feeling at ease with the flow of ideas and images. Knowing a story also involves knowing about its source. Being familiar with where a story comes from, where it might have been heard and who might have told it, helps retold stories come alive. Telling a story involves a variety of techniques and skills, and changes of character and involves the listeners too.

Assuming the mantle of traditional storytellers can bring meaning and enjoyment to the use of stories in primary geography, particularly where they draw upon beliefs and attitudes towards the environment found in different parts of the world.

Children's viewpoints

Adult perspectives on the world differ from the way children encounter and experience their surroundings. Many children first meet this diversity through stories. Later, it may come through school links with children elsewhere and talks with classroom visitors. Primary geography offers scope for exploring how people give different meaning to places. Discovering how places are

understood and valued helps children to appreciate how the world is perceived differently. They too recognise the importance of being able to respond in different ways. Depending on a person's experience, observable facts can give different meanings and result in very different interpretations. Meeting these different perspectives in stories stimulates the children's own thinking. Combining subjective and imaginative thinking with objective observation is central to geographical understanding, as it helps children to interpret facts, to solve problems and to make informed judgements.

Our town 1912

Our town 1993

ACTIVITIES

As many activities share the same practical considerations, a general set of headings applies:

Objective
To encourage geographical skills and understanding through story-related activities.

Age range
All ages.

Group size
Whole class, individuals and groups.

What you need
Suitable stories with a geographical interest (see Chapter 15) and supplementary pictures; maps, writing and drawing materials, flip chart for word bank, cameras (if appropriate), tape recorder, reference materials, cardboard boxes, programmable toys, floor mats or play maps, travel bag and items to pack in it, atlases, outline maps, wall maps, photocopiable page 190.

1. Stories in pictures

Retell a story using pictures. Ask the children to look closely for clues and features about the story in the pictures. Ask them where the people, creatures or objects are and what activities are taking place. Get them to point to parts of the pictures which illustrate any movement between different parts of the story. Look for hidden parts of the story. What might be hidden from view? Who or what else might be in the picture? How might other scenes in the story be illustrated? How might the final scene be shown if the last page was missing? Introduce geographical terms wherever appropriate.

Ask the children to map the landscape described in the story. They can map where the characters go in the story and sequence places they pass. Could they go anywhere else? Could they make any other decisions? Might the story end in a different way? How might the story be different if another character from the same or different story went too? How might the journey in the story change? Would they stop at different places, follow a different route or travel at a different speed?

The children can draw pictures (or take photographs) to retell the story in a place they know well. The pictures and text can be sequenced together, and captions printed using the computer. How might they tell this story to someone who could not see the pictures?

Ask the children what kinds of sounds they might hear in the places shown in these pictures. They could record or improvise a sound-track for the story which captures the sense of the place. You could ask them if any other senses could be used in responding to the picture. Does it remind them of any distinctive taste or smell?

Ask the children if they think the story is set in a real place. Can they find other pictures of that place? Get them to compare their pictures with those in the book. What different things are shown? If the story is set in an imaginary place, ask the children to find pictures of places which look like it. Has the writer or artist disguised a real place or

revealed clues about where the place is? You could also make a word list which identifies similarities and differences in the story and a more familiar place.

2. Stories in journeys

Ask the children to work out the route of a journey described in a story and then fill in photocopiable page 190. Encourage them to act out parts of the story using toys and suitable background settings (floor mats, or play maps, or the children could box-model part of the setting and draw their own outline plan. They could also use programmable toys to depict parts of the journey (see Chapter 10). If they trace the journey on a floor mat they could decide where sign posts or clues could mark the route. You could ask them if they had only three way-markers where would they put them, or if they could mark their route in other ways without spoiling the place for others.

Ask the children to compare the setting or journey with the local area or a similar journey.

A small group of children could pack a bag with things they would need to take on the journey. They could also keep a travel log for the characters on their journey. Some children could locate places in the story on a map or globe. Ask them how they would reach the place in the story if they were actually going there. How would they travel? Where would they go and in which direction? Encourage the children to plan an itinerary and work out distances, places to stop, points they might pass on the way and so on.

Some children could research how the story travelled to the classroom. Where did it originally come from? Where did the writer and illustrator come from? How did it arrive in the classroom?

The story could be related to a wall map. Some children could research where other stories come from, and where most and least stories come from. They could map an A to Z of stories from around the world. They could research the main characters in stories from different parts of the world and discover if some countries far apart have similar stories.

Ask the children to retell a story in their own words. They could find pictures to illustrate it and locate any places mentioned on a map or maps. Could the story happen in a place they know?

3. The character in the story

The children could devise a day in the life of a character in a story. They could write about the places they might visit, the people they might meet, what happened and so on, over a twenty-four hour period. You could then discuss with them how this daily routine compares with their own lifestyle.

Some children might like to write a letter or diary entry which reflects the hobbies or interests of the character or records a memorable occasion in that particular place (using evidence from the story and elsewhere).

They might like to write a biography for one character, spanning their lives so far or projecting into the future (using evidence from the story and elsewhere).

The children could decide on a set of ten principles by which their favourite character could try to improve the world, the country or where they live. They could then suggest how different characters might seek to change where they live if they had the means. What would be their priorities in making where they live a better place? What difficulties might they meet in bringing about these changes?

Ask the children to imagine themselves in the story. What might they most or least enjoy about being in this place or on this journey? What would they most or least miss about their present lifestyle if they were in the setting of the story?

Ask the children to address a postcard to someone at a place in this story. How might it travel? They could plot its route and investigate how long the journey might take. What might the picture show and what might be written on the reverse side?

Discuss with the children which character in the story they would most like to interview. What questions would they ask? How could

they find out more about the lifestyle of characters in the story and where they live? As a media reporter what types of scenes would be most representative of where and how the people in the story lived? They could research and illustrate scenes not featured in the story. What features might they include?

• Where a story involves an environmental issue you could focus on the conflicting viewpoints, human activities or responses to the events (such as hurricanes, floods, earthquakes, forest fires, avalanches or drought). Social issues may be suitable starting points to develop from stories too, such as a family losing their main source of income, migrating in search of work, getting to know new neighbours, or the threat of

development. You could supplement the story with details from other sources.
• The children could model scenes or buildings where the action of the story takes place. They could devise a stage set where the scenes could be improvised, scripted or recorded using a video camera.
• Alternative ends to the story could be explored by computer modelling, creative writing or through role-play.
• Encourage the children to contact outside agencies by writing letters, inviting speakers or meeting people who have real experiences similar to those in the story. You could get the children to host debates or public enquiries to relate the imaginative situation to real-world circumstances.

Reflections

Approaching geography through story is a way of developing the children's world-view. Any locational framework should include places encountered through stories as they help to foster children's curiosity about their own changing world. Stories furnish additional images which make sense of the complexities and contradictions surrounding us and connect the present to the past and future. They may help to confront stereotyping, reinforce new understandings and extend children's geographical experience in meaningful ways. They have considerable value with all ability ranges and

particular relevance for children with special needs.

Ideally, all stories should be related to their original contexts. Whether starting from contemporary or traditional stories, it is advisable to try to provide a background so that the meaning and significance of the story becomes clearer to the children. Stories from traditional sources require not only details about the traditional ways of life, but also, wherever possible, information about contemporary lifestyles too. Likewise stories about places in the past require setting beside modern images and impressions of places, so that neither people nor places are seen as an unchanging museum

exhibit. Displays, presentations, school visits and contacts with appropriate government and non-governmental agencies help to raise children's awareness of contemporary lifestyles and geographical or environmental change.

Meeting the stories of others, may help children to see how the inner and outer worlds of experience interrelate. If their role as listeners to other people's stories and points of view can bring new awareness and meaning, perhaps they can also become storytellers and help to promote a sense of understanding, appreciation and responsibility for the places and peoples around them.

CHAPTER 9

Visual clues

Visual messages constantly surround us and affect our experience of the contemporary world. Learning how to decode the myriad pictures, symbols and fragmented images which influence how we see and interpret, is a necessary part of our personal survival kit. Whether trying to work out road signs at a junction ahead, wiring a plug or watching news on television, visual literacy is an integral part of everyday living for the majority of people.

The highly visual nature of modern communication and human activity has several important implications for geographical education. Geography is a very visual subject and responds to observable reality or representations of that reality. Whether the children are reading a landscape or a map, vision usually plays an important part in the perception, analysis and interpretative processes. The very substance of much geographical interest frequently comes into children's lives through images and pictures in recollected, printed and broadcast form.

Direct encounters with virtual reality on screen or through interactive simulations sometimes make it difficult for the children to distinguish between indirect and real experiences. Even real travel experiences on actual journeys can be seen through eyes and expectations affected by photographic images and views seen beforehand. Learning to see without viewing through the eyes of a camera is therefore important if children are to understand and respond in meaningful ways to their surroundings. This chapter explores how greater visual awareness and criticality not only assist children's skills in observation and recording, but enrich perception and geographical understanding.

BACKGROUND

Since decoding visual messages is strengthened by involving children as image makers, the widening access to video and still-camera now opens up exciting opportunities for primary geography. The following sections suggest how different kinds of visual image may be used in geography and offer some reminders about image and picture interpretation. There are hints on basic camera work, storyboarding and management tips on how to organise children as image-makers (both in school and on location). As the practical tips on working with cameras are transferable to a wide variety of geographical investigations and fieldwork settings, possible uses are also found in other chapters and the activities section focuses on the use of still photographs in geographical contexts.

Looking for visual clues

Looking at images is not always easy; sometimes the viewer has to work quite hard to discover what the image-maker is trying to show. We need to think about the actual process of making the picture and the relationship of its maker to the subject matter. We might question why the artist has selected that viewpoint, the particular weather conditions and the foreground or background details.

We might think about how the subject matter, as well as the use of light or colour, affect the overall mood of the picture. Observable patterns, repeated shapes, a sense of movement or rhythm, and the use of space, may influence our own responses to a landscape or urban scene. Sometimes the intensity of feeling captured in a particular painting extends into how the artist has applied the paint and style of brushwork. At other times, our responses are evoked less by what the painting depicts, than by the associations it brings to mind. Encouraging children to see creative work in two- and three-dimensional form (as alternative ways of understanding places) does not reduce art to a source of evidence, but additionally opens up other ways of finding geographical meaning and appreciation.

When looking at photographs, videos or films which show people and places, we should encourage children to ask what is and what is not depicted by the camera. Only through such questions can they find the underlying stories that pictures can tell. When looking at images we should think about why some, rather than other views, are represented and what is left out of sight. We might wonder if people in photographs knew and agreed to being recorded. We might compare scenes and photographs to other images and impressions, from similar places and situations. By questioning not only what can be seen in an image, but also how and why it shows particular things, introduces children to different ways of looking at familiar (and yet often neglected) images in the world around them.

Looking for meaning

Images are excellent starting points in discussions about places and lifestyles. Taking a closer look not only practises observation skills, but enriches perception and understanding. Sometimes different layers of meaning can be peeled away from a picture. Finding ways to uncover these hidden messages is appropriate, whether working with visual evidence produced in school or from a variety of other sources. Various aspects of interpretation implicitly inform and prompt how we encourage children to look at pictures. Various types of questions we can use are listed below:
• What is going on? What is the apparent meaning?
• What's going on beneath the surface? What else may be happening, represented, referred to or in the minds of people shown in the scene? Does it echo or refer to well-known stories, gestures, situations or significant events?
• Why does it look like this? What is the significance of the

way the picture has been framed? What might the photographer have left out of view? Do people know or approve the fact that their pictures are being taken?
• What does it personally mean? Does it have any special meaning, provoke any strong feelings or suggest anything, anyone or anywhere in particular?
• Does it have a wider meaning? What else might be associated with it (objects, sounds, smells, atmosphere, places)?

Such questions may be talking points or prompt further investigation. They may be used in a number of the suggested activities, but it would be rather indigestible to attempt them all at the same time!

Working with cameras

Cameras are tools for gathering information, recording and analysing, and for sharing findings. Their images (either singly or in sequence) generally reflect the purpose of the person behind the camera. Children should undertake photographic enquiries as part of geographical investigation with

clear intentions in mind. However, whether taken by experts or beginners, photographs have a habit of being unpredictable and capturing the unexpected!

Expensive equipment needs to be used with care and economy. Although children are increasingly familiar with cameras, using a school camera is an important occasion for encouraging considerate behaviour, as well as detailed observation. While some children may take their own cameras on school visits, camera-work in the local environment is usually best attempted using school equipment.

Any equipment should be introduced and explained before venturing outside. The photographic work to be done should also be discussed. Recording sheets should be explained beforehand and the allocation of children to take turns in using equipment, writing notes or carrying materials should all be agreed in advance.

Preparation should include tips on being a considerate photographer. Photographing scenes is generally much less intrusive than taking individual views of people,

personal belongings and private homes or places (where it is customary to seek approval before beginning photography). Learning to be a sensitive photographer introduces an awareness about other people's pictures which children meet in printed and broadcast form.

When viewing the world through a camera lens it is easy to ignore personal safety. Children should use a camera only when they are stationary and avoid looking through the view-finder when moving. They should be aware of the hazards around them and responsible for each other's safety, acting as lookouts while others take pictures. Photographic safaris can become risky activities if the children are not able to take on shared responsibility.

Limiting children to work with a specific number of exposures encourages selecting views carefully and helps to avoid unnecessary shots. An initial survey could identify the best views and then the shots could be selected from a shortlist. Each child should take a certain number of photographs so that

Storyboard of Peter, Suzi and Khal's Journey to the Castle

photographs may then be taken in any order (see 'Using a camcorder' on this page). A series of stages are evident in carrying out a photographic survey and may be expressed as questions:
• What is our overall purpose?
• Where should we go to take our photographs?
• What do we want our pictures to show?
• What is our total number of exposures and how should be best use them?
• Which views are most suitable for our purpose?
• Does our survey need images to begin, end or locate the sequence?

Discussion and decisions should accompany every stage to help the children to tackle camera-work in a thoughtful and purposeful manner. If the photographs are to tell a narrative, it may be helpful to first devise a storyboard.

Using a storyboard

A storyboard is a base for enabling photographic images to tell a story. It is an effective framework for selecting a limited number of camera shots to introduce, extend and tell a story or put across a series of ideas in sequence. The narrative may be simple and straightforward, or build up a series of increasingly complex images or impressions. A storyboard can be purely visual or add words and sounds.

Storyboards may also act as a log for each photograph, recording details of the underlying idea as well as who was the photographer, where and when it was taken and any other incidental information. Storyboards may provide a basis for follow-up investigation or composing a simple commentary to accompany the photographs. Recording ensures a systematic approach, encourages equal involvement in the activity and gives children not actually taking photographs other important active roles. You find it a useful means of monitoring activity which is not directly supervised by you, particularly if this is taking place in small groups in the school grounds or off-site with adult support.

Using a camcorder

As camcorders and video cameras gain in popularity, opportunities for working with moving images continue to grow. Wider access to equipment make it appropriate to consider the application of camcorders to geographical investigation, although some of the basic considerations for camera work of any kind still apply (so this section should be read in conjunction with 'Working with cameras', on page 117).

Camcorders record and present information about the school or locality in an immediate and visual way. Children must work with each other and with the equipment in a responsible way. Camcorders also encourage technical competency and invite critical viewing of both the subject matter and the recorded image. The children can evaluate the camera-work when the memories are still fresh in their minds and this can often reach a rigour hard to find in direct criticism of each other's work. Follow-up work to overcome problems is much easier than when working with still-cameras, as the film can be re-used.

Many aspects of working with a camcorder are not dissimilar from using still-cameras. Children should be familiar with their equipment, working brief, storyboarding and safety procedure before leaving the classroom. Group members may take on several additional roles, such as look-outs during filming for people, animals or vehicles (which may interrupt recording). A body-guard might oversee the film-maker's safety, in relation to traffic and pedestrians. A time-keeper may monitor the length of shots to ensure views are not too short. Storyboarding and carrying of equipment are also vital roles which should be shared.

Teamwork is essential at every stage and in all decisions. The initial survey of the filming location should involve everyone and use all their suggestions. Selecting shots and putting them in sequence are important in basic video work. Getting the order wrong leads to complicated editing, or re-doing the entire sequence of shots! If the sequence of shots is decided before beginning to film, it makes editing much easier. Careful storyboarding should identify the sequence of the shots and once agreed should be followed. The following tips on working with a camcorder may be useful.

• *Avoid filming into the sun.*
• *Move the camera between shots rather than during shots; for instance, avoid too much zooming in and out in each shot.*
• *Avoid trying to film while on the move: it is not very effective!*
• *Avoid composing views with objects at different distances (unless you want a blurred image). Cameras need to have one specific feature to focus on unless they are very sophisticated.*

Camcorders are quite sensitive to sound, so children need to be as quiet as possible during filming. Background sounds can give a sense of place unless they are interrupted by the film crew! With practice and a script, children may attempt a spoken commentary during filming, although it is usually better to involve someone other than the person filming. Spoken commentaries should not merely repeat what the camera shows and they are often better left until children are

more competent in working with a camera. Wind, traffic and unwanted sounds can drown children's voices when recorded on location. A synchronised tape-recording composed back in the classroom or a live commentary are effective alternatives. Background music is possible, although children should recognise that their choice of sound will affect the overall impression and mood that their images give.

Awareness of such technical details may make working with camcorders seem more complicated than it really is. A trial lesson in the playground should help the children to gain a basic competence, as long as they are all able to handle the equipment, attempt some filming and discuss their efforts afterwards. Technicalities should not obscure the purpose of using camcorders in geographical investigation. Their use may bring new skills and ways of working together, but should also provide alternative means for responding to observable evidence.

ACTIVITIES

As many activities share the same practical considerations, a general set of headings applies:

Objective
To encourage observation skills and investigation through using varied kinds of pictures and photographs in different ways.

Age range
All ages.

Group size
Small groups or individuals (unless very large photographs or prints are available for class demonstration and discussion).

What you need
A wide range of photographs, postcards and pictures of scenes which show places, peoples and geographical issues in contrasting localities. Sources might include aerial photographs, old and recent images from public and private sources (including local history or newspaper archives, planning departments, estate agents, family photographs, pictures from tourist publications and posters, guides, books, calendars); writing paper, art materials, scissors, acetate sheets and pens, cameras, maps, clip-boards and cassette recorders, the Braille alphabet. Note: Paintings, prints and drawings by different artists could be used in many of the following activities in similar ways.

1. Describing photographs

Select a photograph and brainstorm with the children on word associations suggested by it. Identify any geographical words and features that they mention and create a word bank for future reference.

Ask the children to select a photograph of a particular scene. Then ask them to write about why they chose that picture and any interesting or unusual features in it. Does it remind them of anything or anywhere else? Can they find out where this photograph was taken? Why might it have been taken?

Ask a group of children to develop an easy-to-use filing system for picture resources or postcards. Then ask them to attach to each one printed word lists for independent investigation and creative writing activities.

Mount a photograph on paper and ask a group of children to jot down as many questions as they can around the border. (They can indicate with arrows but avoid drawing them on the actual print.) Alternatively, they can use an acetate overlay so that lines can be drawn from the questions to the picture. Use the questions as a basis for discussion with the children, raising awareness of issues or further investigation possibilities.

Give a group of children one or more pictures; ask the children to write captions for them. They can then compare these with the original captions (if known). Mount a temporary exhibition.

Ask the children to write descriptions to accompany one or more photographs, with different audiences in mind. Get them to describe the photographs as precisely as they can. Then get them to devise simple captions to convert into Braille or another language (if appropriate).

Some children may like to make a sketch of a photograph and label with geographical terms using the word bank. A simple pre-drawn grid (on acetate) laid over the photograph will help them make an accurate version.

2. Putting time into photographs

Discuss a photograph with the children and get them to imagine that it is a frozen moment in time; a second before or after, and it would have been slightly different. Encourage them to write about any changes they might see if it were part of a film being wound forward (or backwards) to reveal later or earlier frames.

Choose some photographs which show plenty of human activity (or features) which might be different at other times. Ask the children to write a diary entry which fits the scene and then another entry for a different time.

Choose some photographs which show at least one person in them. Then ask the children to devise some bubble-writing to express the thoughts and speech of the person(s) at the time when the picture was taken. They could write a conversation between people in the picture, or between the person in the picture and the one taking the photograph (or an imaginary person).

Give the children a selection of photographs showing different activities. Ask them to write a day in the life of a person or a place using these photographs to offer suggestions of different activities. With the help of additional information, you can also get them to devise a lifestyle chart showing a person's whereabouts and activities during a twenty-four hour period. They can then compare this lifestyle chart with their own personal lifestyle chart.

3. Soundtrack of photographs

Ask the children to imagine that a photograph has a soundtrack. What noises or sounds might be heard in this scene or landscape? Does the scene or landscape suggest any particular taste, or smell or evoke any other sensory response?

emphasised? How might the photographs promote one of these aspects?

4. Similar and different

Show the children a photograph and ask them if they have ever been to, seen or read about places which look like the one in the photograph? Can they find out where the photograph was taken? Does the photograph remind them of any dream, experience or memory?

Ask the children to compare old and new photographs of places taken from the same viewpoint. Get them to look for differences and annotate or write about noticeable changes. They could then investigate why certain changes have occurred.

5. Advertising gloss

Give a small group of children four photographs of particular places and ask them to devise some 'advertising gloss' for these localities. Which aspects should be most or least

6. Drama from a photograph

Give the children some photographs as a starting point for a play. They can improvise the dialogue and script, and record it, or set it to sound. Alternatively, they could use them as bases for creative movement, dance and mime.

7. Sending a postcard

Give the children some postcards from different places. Get them to use an atlas to find out where the postcards were sent from and how might they reach their destinations. If the postcard could describe its journey what might it recount? What message could have been written on the reverse side? Who might have sent the postcard and why was this place visited? What clues might the postcard picture show?

8. Poems from photographs

Discuss some photographs with the children. Do the photographs show features with clear outlines? If there seems to be a dominant shape in one scene, ask them to draw it faintly in pencil on paper and get them to write a poem in that shape. Then get them to experiment with shape poems as frameworks for writing in a way which captures the essence of the scene (or landscape) shown in a photograph.

Ask the children to write a poem about a place or scene in a photograph. They could list seven features or things connected with the scene and put each on a new line, and then develop the description of each listed item by adding words and phrases. The poem should capture the essence of the place. This activity could be tried on recall after visits to actual places.

9. Bird's-eye view

The children could compare an aerial photograph with other photographs of a scene or landscape. Get them to first identify features which are visible in both types of photograph, and then identify features on photographs which do not appear on aerial views.

Show the children a photograph which shows a wide scene or landscape. Get them to suggest what a passenger in a low-flying aircraft might see when looking out from a window at the scene. Get them to think about which features might be easy and hard to see from up in the air.

10. Characteristics of places

The children could make a montage of images which reflect all the different characteristics of a particular place they know well. They could add additional freehand sketches, if necessary. Then they could compare their impression of the local area with other people's views.

Ask the children to compare types of landmarks, street furniture and features found in photographs of different places. They could sort them into types using headings such as: old, new, natural and human-made. What distinctive landmarks can they find where they live? What other features give a place character or identity? They could design their own landmark for where they live. Some children could also make a photo-survey of distinctive features in contrasting places.

11. Taking photographs

Encourage the children to take photographs to show how local places, buildings and features have wider world connections. (Materials, design, decoration, designers, artists, and function might offer clues). They could then make a chart (or use a wall map) to show these links with other places.

Record land-use around the school by getting the children to take photographs. Get them to look for clues of human activity and natural processes in their pictures. They could then label and mount the photographs linking them to a local map.

Ask the children to take some photographs of places and buildings from unusual viewpoints. They could also draw any fantastical creatures, faces, shapes and patterns they discover in the buildings of the local area. These can be located on a local map, or the children could design their own map of the local bestiary. They could make an illustrated guide for the visitor interested in fantasy travel. They should give clear directions and include tips for best viewing times and other practicalities! Go on a local photo-safari with the children and focus on

Indian name

satellite dish

telephone wires

African carving

foreign languages

Yucca plant

left hand drive

French sign

a particular theme, for instance, gateways, old walls, patterns, shop signs, trees. Investigate why differences occur and get the children to explore images through art or writing. They could also classify and map the places where the different photographs were taken.

Record wide-angle views with the children by taking a series of overlapping photographs which combine to give a horizontal or vertical scene. These photographs could be compared with a series of linked sketches of the same view, or a transect drawing. The photographs could be mounted on paper and then annotated or related to a local map.

12. Make a jigsaw

Mount some large photographic views, cover them with protective film, and cut them into interlocking jigsaw pieces. For each photograph, write the letters of the place-name on the back of individual jigsaw pieces for the children to unscramble, with the complete name on one of the pieces. You could make a word version, by writing words associated with the photograph on the jigsaw pieces. You can use place jigsaws with children at the start of an activity, to raise awareness of different places. Older children could devise place jigsaws for younger children. Try to encourage word associations which avoid stereotyped images of places.

Reflections

Working with pictures and images offers considerable scope in primary geography and develops valuable skills for living in the contemporary world. Searching for meaning clearly involves children in both using other people's images and learning to become image-makers. Application to both fieldwork and classroom-based activities is evident throughout this chapter, as are the clear links with other areas of the primary curriculum.

Encouraging children as image-makers offers interesting new possibilities for the exchange of environmental and geographical information between schools. Written work and drawings have long been shared between some schools, providing valuable insights into other places through the eyes and thoughts of young observers. Wider access to photographic equipment now brings more scope for sharing images of different localities.

Sharing visual information which accurately reflects lifestyle and locality can overcome language barriers. Exchanging a photographic survey of school and lifestyle (or even a video) is practical where access to equipment and compatible video recording systems are possible. A project in which children make a survey about themselves and their locality clearly links geography to other areas of the curriculum. Whilst creating a unique teaching resource for others, it would also be a valuable part of their own learning.

Images provide an excellent tool for encouraging language development among bilingual or multilingual children. Meeting scenes and places through pictures, helps children to set their own framework of spatial and social relationships within the wider context of the local area and community. Using everyday scenes and situations gives meaning to new words and experiences. Geographical learning thus encourages children to develop another active vocabulary that links them with their surroundings, without losing the identity which their own accent, dialect or language gives. Primary geography's concern with helping children to locate themselves within the world means that observable evidence and visual clues become powerful tools for encouraging orientation and language acquisition, particularly when working with children of diverse linguistic backgrounds.

CHAPTER 10

Information technology

Living in the age of the micro-chip influences many aspects of daily existence. Wherever we are, databases, programmed machines, games and graphics, calculations and communications are part of an ever-expanding computerised information system. Modern living means that most people are linked into this vast system by some direct or indirect means.

For young children, the world of computers is no more unfamiliar than many other parts of their surroundings. It is a realm to be explored and understood, just like the rest of the world around them. Moreover, the excitement of computer activities often gives them an appeal over other aspects of the children's experiences.

Developing a critical awareness of information technology and its impact upon our thinking, communication, expectation and even our material environment, is an important element of children's learning. Since geography encourages children to make sense of the world around them, it follows that primary geography should help them to make discoveries and develop competence in working with computers.

Since software programs change constantly this chapter focuses on how rather than which programs may be used in the classroom. By drawing attention to the possibilities of using information technology, it is hoped that teachers will then explore how specific programs may contribute to geographical learning in the classroom.

BACKGROUND

Information technology and geography

Strong links exist between information technology and geography at all levels. In the classroom, computers encourage children to handle large data sets, to question and hypothesise, and also to present findings using words, pictures, numbers and graphics. Working with information technology should therefore broaden and complement existing forms of geographical activity.

Much geographical data is well-suited to the computer. Where geography requires children to collect, classify and interpret large quantities of data, computers can help them to store and retrieve the information. Accumulated data on different aspects of the environment may be up-dated so that children appreciate how the knowledge basis itself constantly changes. The speed, flexibility and power of the computer means that children can handle data on a larger scale than ever before. The computer also helps them develop research skills as they begin to look for patterns, trends and meaning in their data.

Many real or imaginary situations offer exciting opportunities for problem-solving and decision-making. Through games and simulations, children can combine various kinds of geographical enquiry with imaginative thinking. As children embark upon these investigations they are taken into other peoples' experiences. These adventures require personal initiative based on critical thinking and informed understanding.

Ideas and data can often be tested and modified repeatedly before they are presented in written, visual or numerical form. On a computer, word processing allows the children to compose, re-draft and edit on screen. Freed from the time-consuming and often laborious process of drawing graphs, diagrams and maps, children can spend longer considering the content and respective merits of different forms of presentation. A computer can enhance the quality of written or drawn presentations, although this is not always the case and the drawing skills of fine motor control and precision do have a place and should not be neglected.

Selecting suitable software

Software suitable for primary geography tends to fall into one of two categories:
• it can either be content-free and open-ended in its application, as exemplified by word processing and desk-top publishing programs, databases, spreadsheets and packages for graphics or statistics; or
• it can be a content-led program, which is less flexible,

but offers discrete and ready planned units of work.

Some pre-school children become familiar with content-led programs, through computer games and simulations. However there are increasing amounts of software available for introducing content-free packages at an early stage, as the following sections will suggest.

Both categories of software have their supporters and critics. Although content-led programs are useful as ready-made activities, their suitability to particular situations may be limited. They may, however, help to introduce keyboard skills and lead on to more stimulating and interactive computing activities. In selecting suitable software the following questions could act as a guide:
• What is its purpose?
• Are its objectives clear?
• Are the values acceptable and appropriate?
• Does the program have a broad or narrow curriculum focus?
• Are the ideas up-to-date and accurate?
• Does the program allow for updating or additional material?
• Does the program require extensive teacher supervision?
• Is the content interesting and stimulating?
• Are the instructions clear and logical?
• Do the instructions offer help and feedback?
• Do they offer encouragement and reinforcement?
• Will the material appeal to the children?
• Will the content and graphics sustain interest?
• Are the colours and sound distracting?
• Is the program suitable for

different age and ability groups?
• Is the level and quality of support materials appropriate?
• Are extension activities included?

Computers and special learning needs

Computers offer children with special learning needs greater independence from the teacher, and scope to try out geographical ideas alone. Activities can enhance self-esteem as children gain a sense of competence and control through following a sequence of instructions. A boost to self-confidence may encourage motivation and concentration, and spark off more positive attitudes towards other activities. Where children with emotional difficulties find relating to other people hard, they may sometimes work successfully with the emotionally more neutral computer.

Computer graphics and repetitive patterns of action and response can sometimes assist the teacher in diagnosing the children's learning needs. A space bar, joy-stick or mouse may be easier for some children than using a pencil. Children with poor coordination can often use concept keyboard overlays, whereby they communicate through simple pictographs or a touchscreen and transmit responses directly to the computer screen. Touchpads which use simple keyboard skills are also available in some of the programmable toys suitable for classroom use.

When working with a computer the teacher should keep a record of how the children acquire, consolidate and extend their social and intellectual skills through information technology. It can be useful to identify those skills which apply to the whole curriculum or to specific subjects. Children can keep their own simple record of programs for self-assessment.

ACTIVITIES

1. Programmable toys

Computer controlled toys may familiarise children with information technology and introduce various geographical concepts. Some toys are little more than a simply programmed touchpad which moves a vehicle around on the floor in response to a series of commands. The value of this equipment in the classroom is sometimes marred by its application to military-style vehicles and their accompanying sound effects. More elaborate programmable toys help young children to develop spatial skills. Two electronic toys are widely available in schools. These are: 'Turtle' gaining its name from its domed back and 'Roamer' which has more canine characteristics!

Objective
To introduce directions, making and using simple maps, route-planning and the principle of programming through programmable toys.

Age range
Five to seven.

Group size
Whole class and small groups (no more than two or three children should work with a programmable toy in the classroom at one time).

What you need
Programmable toys (such as Roamer or Turtle), large sheets of (squared) paper, writing materials, cardboard boxes, construction toys, floor apparatus for more complex route-finding activities, a turtle graphic package (for work on the computer screen).

What to do
In the hall or a large empty space, ask the children to move around by following your instructions. Ensure that they all follow each direction accurately and rapidly. Put them into pairs and ask them to *program* each other by giving simple instructions. Ensure that each child can follow a short route and describe all the moves they make.

In the classroom, tell the children that Turtle and Roamer move in response to similar commands typed in on a keyboard. Ask them to convert their own movements into Roamer or Turtle talk, encourage them to give instructions which control straight-line distances, moves and turns. Some children can be prompted to invent new commands for more complex routes.

Further activities
• Demonstrate how a programmable toy can draw a line as it moves. Record its route using a large sheet of paper. Distribute large sheets of squared paper with pre-drawn axes (marked with letter or number coordinates) for the children to match their programming with the actual route of the toy's journey at different points. Ask pairs of children to give instructions to the toy using the coordinates and then check the accuracy of their programming. Ask them to record how many times the toy stopped in the correct position.
• Ask the children to make the route of their programmable toy more elaborate by adding distances, directions and other information. Encourage them to use cardboard boxes, construction toys or floor apparatus to create additional barriers and features for the programmable toy to negotiate.
• Suggest that the children create an imaginary role for their programmable toy. Ask them to devise instructions which enable the toy to undertake deliveries, shopping trips or more adventurous purposeful missions which take them from point to point along a pre-determined route.
• Introduce children to Turtle graphics so that they can transfer their directional and programming skills from a horizontal to vertical plane. By learning to apply the same principles with a concept keyboard, children can get Turtle to move around on the screen.

2. Maps and co-ordinates

As children develop keyboard skills, various programs offer

interesting map-based
activities which enable them to
explore different kinds of
spatial relationships.

Objective
To introduce children to
simple coordinates and grid
references.

Age range
Seven to eight.

Group size
Individuals, pairs and small
groups.

What you need
A software package which
introduces maps and
coordinates in a game based
on locating a mystery object.

What to do
Discuss with the children the
purpose of the program and
identify any ideas or issues
which may be unfamiliar to
them. Remind the children of
how the program fits into a
wider unit of work (so that the
game does not exclude all
other thoughts).

Ask the children to take
turns at following the
instructions accurately. Get
them to use the instructions to
move around the screen in
their hunt for buried treasure
or a hidden object. Ask them
to practise simple keyboard
commands which allow the
cursor to travel in straight
lines, or make left and right
turns, and plot or follow
routes between different
points. Check that they can
identify direction, position and
movement as they move the
cursor around the screen.

Further activities
• Introduce the children to
simple compass directions
which may or may not be part
of the program. Stick compass
directions to the edge of the
computer screen so that the
children can practise
orientation.
• As children learn to use
coordinates ask them to draw
simple imaginary island maps
for others to explore (either on
the screen or using a print-
out). Ask them in pairs to
devise a set of instructions
which are then used by other
children to find their way to a
particular place. Get them to
imagine that their survival
depends upon being found so
they must give clear
instructions.
• Use a base plan of the school
or playground, or ask the
children to explore and move
around within an outline plan.
Other real or imaginary places
can also prompt various route-
finding activities once the
children have had some
experience of using plans and
directions. Basic mapping
skills can also be introduced
using programmable floor toys.
• Adventure and simulation
packages provide scope for
mapping tasks too (see 'Using
local maps', page 130). For
instance, there are programs
which ask the children to take
vehicles through checkpoints
on a car rally, chart sea
voyages across treacherous
stretches of water, or plot a
series of deliveries between
different places without
running out of petrol (and
other problem-solving
situations).

3. Using local maps

Objective
To transfer information from maps into a database (on a grid by grid basis) and to practise retrieval skills.

Age range
Nine to eleven.

Group size
Individuals, pairs and whole class. (Typing data into the computer works well with groups of three: children read, enter and check for accuracy).

What you need
Large scale local maps (several copies for reference), mapping program, writing materials, copies of earlier print outs or previous databases (for comparison). When linked to fieldwork, observations, photographs and recorded information are necessary.

What to do
Select a large scale map of the local area (or an area with which the children are familiar). Ask them what information they can read from the map. List on the board the map coordinates for each feature they identify. Use the map coordinates to mark the position of features on a mapping grid displayed on the screen.

Further activities
The children could discuss how to develop a particular location as a leisure park or bakery. Ask the children in groups to list points to consider in selecting a suitable site. Ask them to discuss alternative locations and identify the merits of each site. Using a large scale map (or street plan) as a concept keyboard overlay (see 'Concept keyboard page 132), ask each group to mark their preferred site on the overlay. They should enter their preferences for each site into a database of possible locations. The groups might then discuss these different sites.

4. Databases

Fieldwork observation is ideal for work on databases (weather, rocks, soils, waterways, vegetation, land-use, buildings, homes, traffic, shops and other places of work and leisure). Opportunities for data handling are provided by census data, aspects of the school site, school records, and of course, the children themselves.

Objective
To introduce children to database software. To indicate how to store and use information about a certain subject in a structured way.

Age range
All ages.

Group size
Individuals, pairs and the whole class. (Spread the task of entering the data between children in groups of three.)

What you need
Fieldwork data, suitable database program.

What to do
This activity should be part of another one involving the collection of information. To begin with, the children need to identify the information they wish to gather and how they are to collect it. Discuss with them the type of information they require and then help them to classify it using headings.

Use the software instructions to create a file for the children to type their data into the computer. Ask them to sort their data first and then enter the information into the program according to pre-agreed headings. As this stage can be time-consuming, put the children into groups of three to enter and store the data, and then rotate the groups.

Once data is stored, discuss with the children how they can interrogate the information.

They must decide how to question to achieve a result and which questions to ask. Allow them time to sort through the material themselves and to try different data retrieval routes by looking at more than one heading. Encourage them to follow hunches which may lead on to new enquiries. Ask them to spot patterns and to look for contrasts, comparisons and other relationships. Set up hypotheses which can be tested, changed or discarded.

Further activities
• Once the data has been carefully classified by the children along pre-determined lines, they should be able to interpret and present their findings using diagrams, graphs, maps or word-processing packages.
• The children can update or add information about particular investigations from time to time. They can also use a pre-existing file to work with information that has already been collected and sorted.

5. Quizzes and questions

Objective
To use a database in conjunction with a quiz program, to devise a simple information-based game. Keyboard and data-handling skills can be practised informally.

Age range
Nine to eleven.

Group size
Pairs.

What you need
Content-free quiz package, reference books (to help them compile precise and accurate databases).

What to do
Select a quiz package which is content-free (so that the children can enter their own information and questions). Ask the children to key in simple questions about their data. The children can create a multiple-choice quiz and even score using the computer.

6. Profiles and transects

Objective
To use graphics to record and present the findings of a profile or transect as a follow-up to fieldwork.

Age range
Seven and over.

Group size
Small groups as part of a wider class activity (although the task may involve a general discussion involving all the children).

What you need
Database program (which constructs profiles and transects) and spreadsheets (useful for presenting information in other ways).

What to do
Discuss with the children which fieldwork data might help to construct a transect of buildings along a street on the computer. Put the children into threes and ask them to enter the data (for example, the width, height or number of floors and the use for each surveyed building). Use the information to draw a transect on the computer.

Further activities
• If an area is surveyed gradually or revisited regularly, get the children to monitor change through time by keeping and comparing the diagrams printed at different stages of data collection.
• Ask the children to print out graphics for displays or class-produced books and newspapers on topical issues and the local area.
• If your class is linking with another elsewhere, discuss with the children how they might present information about themselves and their locality in graphical form (particularly if language difficulties are involved).

Concept keyboard

The concept keyboard is one of the most versatile computer applications in the classroom, particularly when working with young children (or those with special learning needs). Essentially, it is a flat overlay for the computer keyboard which can be programmed so that whole words, sentences or images are entered or accessed at a single touch. A number of programs may be used with a concept keyboard and their software includes samples of overlays and files.

In geography, the concept keyboard may be used as a simple database, an introduction to basic shape and directional work. It also offers scope for writing, poster design and caption writing. These possibilities may be taken further as the children enter topics of their own choice into the overlay framework and create files for their own needs.

Simulations

Computer simulations can open doors to worlds of geographical experiences which real-world constraints of time, money and practicalities deny. Through imaginative thinking, children can explore a range of experiences and situations in different parts of

the world. Most simulations put children into real or fictional situations from which they have to extract themselves, by making informed decisions and solving problems. Some packages require them to become familiar with a range of relevant information and then offer insights into specific geographical situations.

Geographical simulations are plentiful within available software and may prompt more able children to tackle real-world problems. Many geographical themes provide the necessary tension and problem-solving situation which a simulation requires. Some examples of real world simulations are:

• *local themes*: planning a traffic by-pass, building a new town, designing a shopping centre, developing a mining concession, flooding a valley, polluting a pond, protecting a threatened conservation area, running a profitable farm, and organising a fishing fleet;

• *other localities*: processes of environmental change (dune movement and farming in arid lands), population growth and resource issues, real environmental events (eruptions, floods, earthquakes or tornadoes), past explorers' journeys, and some of the other themes listed under local themes.

The simulations may function as adventure games and invite fantasy and speculation. They may also be set within real contexts at various scales and prompt the children to additional research before they decide upon an agreed course of action. Geography-led simulations can involve children in considerable amounts of purposeful discussion, analytical thinking and synthesis, and lead into other cross-curricular activities. These packages are usually popular with children and can become a basis for a considerable amount of related work.

Computer modelling

Computer models help the children to investigate various geographical situations. In each case, children analyse the data to discover patterns and relationships and establish the underlying geographical processes. They then use this to predict what might happen when the conditions alter or when the process continues for a long period of time.

Models are more generalised situations where neither the teacher, nor outside constraints, limit the possibilities for decision-making, testing suppositions and open-ended speculation. Computer models extend the data and encourage the children to predict the future from existing trends. Sometimes they speed up processes of change which occur over very long time-scales.

Within physical geography, children may investigate how cave systems form, volcanic landscapes develop, vegetation changes through time, the effects of air pollution on plant cover or building materials. In human geography contexts, children might explore why a settlement grows in a particular way, why people move homes, why transport systems are constructed along specific routes, or what might happen to farmers in successive years of crop failure. Models, just like simulations, may be applied to real or fictitious situations although they tend to simplify reality.

Displaying information

The computer's ability to display information in graphical form makes it an important tool for geographers. Databases yield lists of information which may be sorted into numerical or alphabetical form and plotted as diagrams, bar charts or histograms, pie charts, line graphs or scatter graphs. These activities enable children to present similar data in different ways and evaluate alternative tabular and graphic forms. The speed of drawing computer graphics makes it possible for the children to use sophisticated techniques usually restricted to older age ranges.

Word processing

Word processing is invaluable in the communication of geographical ideas and information. Software packages can help the children to organise, develop and present geographical material using text and image in different ways. There is enormous scope for children to become familiar with many different written forms, from factual environmental reports to letter writing, and from journalism and advertising to creative prose and poetry. Geographical contexts allow the children to write for different audiences and purposes.
• Whether dealing with real or imaginary situations, written work which looks professional and authentic enhances the significance of geographical enquiry. A number of word processing programs include style sheets which allow the text to be set out in different ways. Children value this extra quality in their completed presentations, particularly when working on a letter, pamphlet, advertisement or newspaper.

Electronic mailing

Another important opportunity for geographical enquiry lies in the development electronic mailing (or E-mail systems) which enable children to link up with elsewhere. Attaching a modum to the computer connects them to the local telephone system and, for the cost of a local call, exchanges of information can be made between children in different countries.

Facsimile

Rapid exchange of both text and visual material between children in different places is made possible where the school has its own fax machine or access to one in a local business or organisation. Photographs, drawings, maps and written work can be shared in this way, without sending the originals. The immediacy of this exchange and its technical novelty compensate for its relatively poor reproduction quality and secondhand nature.

Reflections

Information technology supports the children's geographical enquiries into the ever-changing world around them. Geography can help to foster children's awareness of data-handling possibilities and the potential role of technology in their own lives. For teachers too, computer bring unprecedented access to geographical information, resource-based learning and an opportunity for high quality curriculum development.

Working with computers is an important part of the modern primary curriculum. Computers offer children the chance to develop specific geographical and more general skills. They provide another element of variety within a subject which readily lends itself to many exciting cross-curricular approaches. The next few chapters show how these opportunities can be taken further to create a dynamic and memorable curriculum.

CHAPTER 11

Cross-curricular connections

Making sense of the world as a young child involves finding ways to fit together a vast array of disparate thoughts, words, images, experiences, sensations and situations. Out of this confusion children gradually form notions about who and where they are and what seems to go on in the world around them. This learning process uses developing skills, senses and sensibilities.

As children go through school, this unified learning gradually fragments and another landscape of ideas takes its place. The learning environment acquires structures which divide once-united realms of experience and understanding, makes some more important than others, introduces newcomers and sees the disappearance of others. Old alliances go as ways of working, understanding and knowledge become appropriated by subjects which jostle to assert their intellectual credentials in the world of formal learning.

Finding a balance between integrated and separate subject approaches is a recurring educational debate and merit may be found in both sides of the argument.

There is no reason, however, why a primary curriculum with clearly recognisable areas of study should not still provide children with coherent learning experiences which bring together different subjects and cross-curricular working methods. Relevant subject combinations remain effective ways of teaching and learning which avoid imposing a compartmentalised world view, if they are underpinned by planning and a sense of providing structured curriculum opportunities throughout the primary phase.

BACKGROUND

Geography and the wider curriculum

Much evidence points to the educational value of using a variety of different skills and approaches in children's learning. The cross-curricular process is two-way. Insights, knowledge and understanding brought from one area can illuminate, extend and motivate learning elsewhere. It is important, therefore, to provide opportunities which combine different areas of the curriculum, while remembering the undeniable value of sometimes teaching as a discrete subject. Combined approaches and cross-curricular activities may

be a realistic apportionment of time and resources, when schools are squeezing more and more into the primary timetable.

Geography is, by nature, an inter-disciplinary area of study. Many diverse skills, perspectives and knowledge inform how geographers perceive, analyse and interpret the world. Indeed, it is unlikely that much geographical work at any level takes place without making connections with other subject areas. Finding opportunities to link primary geography with other curriculum areas is straightforward, once the specific contributions of individual subjects are identified. Some of the possibilities for cross-curricular approaches are explored in the following sections.

Linking with English

Children's use of language is integral to geographical investigation. It underpins how they plan, develop and present their ideas at all stages, and evaluate their own and others' work. Geography provides varied contexts in which children can become competent as they learn to talk, listen, read and write in acceptable ways, which should enrich both geographical understanding and language development.

The stimulus for much language work comes from how children perceive, interpret and understand their surroundings and themselves. Geography widens opportunities for investigative and creative responses, through enabling children to work and meet people in different situations. Problem-solving and practical activities use language in different written and spoken forms, for varied purposes and audiences. Surveys, interviews and fieldwork involve working with people who may talk and explain in different ways. Children should recognise the importance of clarity, audibility and accuracy in all forms of effective communication. Knowing how to ask and answer questions, devise an enquiry, select useful materials, plan work and interpret information, involves them in discussions and decisions at an individual and collaborative level.

Presenting geographical findings can take varied forms. Spoken presentations may involve reading from notes, talking, debates and discussions, and a number of drama-related activities. Confidence to speak in front of others, stems from being able to talk willingly about things which relate directly to their own experience. As confidence grows, more abstract ideas, areas of understanding and both subjective and objective responses also develop.

Geographical investigation should enable children to share ideas within small and large groups, once they feel confident in themselves and the material they wish to share. Pictures, diagrams, posters, maps, overhead-projector sheets, artefacts and other visual aids or sound cues, are some of the geographical prompts and props which are so valuable in encouraging children to learn to talk and listen.

The quality of children's speech also depends on their listening. Developing attentive ways of listening requires children to recall information, identify other children's presentational strengths or comment upon content or working methods. Listening strengthens children's ability to work with each other and helps them follow the ideas of others. It is sometimes helpful to ask children to brainstorm questions before a visitor arrives and then after the talk to help them focus their pool of queries so that questions assist discussion. The insatiable curiosity of some children may mean that they need no such practice.

Investigation often involves presenting information in written form. Children should have the opportunity to write in different styles and for different audiences and to use word processors. They can present information as letters, journals, scientific or news reports, book reviews, advertisements, descriptions, display panels, notes, planning schemes, guides and trail leaflets, stories, poems and scripts for performance or recording. You need to be clear about how you will assess such material when children's efforts clearly span both geographical understanding and linguistic ability.

Linking with mathematics

Mathematics is one way to view and make sense of the world. As children make mathematical discoveries about their surroundings, they develop geographical awareness too. From an early age, they meet and use numbers in many everyday activities – as they dress, eat or drink, play or listen to songs, rhymes and stories. Numbers form part of the child's observable surroundings, as signs, cars, clothes, houses and many other objects provide information and evidence of activities and patterns in space. Mathematical investigation can thus spark from many aspects of children's lives and interests and also the world around them.

Mathematical skills help children to gather, sort, analyse, interpret and present geographical information. Handling data collected from surveys, questionnaires and other fieldwork activities

requires children to apply mathematical understanding as they search for patterns, trends and spaces.

Number scores help children to collate and record data as they measure and estimate using standard and non-standard units. Calculations require children to add or subtract, multiply and divide in a variety of human, physical or environmental situations. Co-ordinates enable them to present information in graphs and diagrams, and also to draw maps, plans and scale drawings.

Networks help children to follow and devise routes and explore the effects of time, distance and behaviour. Children can apply these ideas in the real world in the planning of journeys and design of trails. Mathematical terms will also help them describe and identify shapes and dimensions in the world around them.

Mathematics provides a systematic and structured basis for investigation and problem-solving in geography. Observations enable children to estimate, predict, test hypotheses and search for alternative outcomes. Practical fieldwork and other geographical activities offer scope for learning to use and apply appropriate materials and skills, including construction kits, drawing instruments, measuring equipment, calculating aids, electronic calculators and other forms of micro-computer. As children develop mathematical competence within geographical contexts, they also practise many other practical, intellectual and social skills.

There is a global dimension to mathematical understanding. Children should recognise that mathematical ideas are expressed in different counting systems, calculating aids and numerical symbols around the world. Studies of

other localities wherever possible should offer children direct experience in these different counting systems. In mathematical terms, this might mean that they set up shop or count using appropriate objects, and solve problems concerning the place and people being studied. Measuring or drawing skills and construction activities might be applied to work with artefacts and pictures of other places. The children can appreciate aspects of other peoples' lifestyle and well-being through comparing price lists or evidence of height, weight and diet.

Geography helps the children to see that mathematical similarities as well as differences exist around the world. The legacy of earlier mathematical ideas might be apparent in the contemporary landscape, particularly where building designs reflect the importance of particular number patterns, ratios and relationships in shape and space. The scale of unfamiliar buildings, settlements or individual possessions, for example, might indicate status and influence over an area. Similar buildings may have different functions and vice versa. Geometrical patterns may offer different clues about beliefs, values and attitudes in other countries and cultural traditions.

Mathematics has informed people's understanding about the world and its people throughout human existence. Finding ways to raise children's awareness of connections between mathematical ideas and geographical thinking can yield exciting and creative cross-curricular work.

Linking with science

Science and geography share a common goal. They both help children to make sense of the world around them through investigations and direct practical involvement. There is considerable overlap in areas of earth science, physical geography and weather studies. Scientific and problem-solving approaches often support geographical investigations, and scientific activities and experiments gain meaning from real-world situations and first-hand experiences.

Investigation requires children to observe, classify, record, hypothesise, experiment and draw inferences from a wide range of environmental evidence. Planning how to investigate, collect and interpret their own set of unique data brings a sense of immediacy and self-worth to children's work in both science and geography. Working in groups, using fieldwork equipment, taking decisions, trying alternative strategies and reaching conclusions in scientific and geographical investigations all involve many practical, social and intellectual skills.

Much primary science starts from a consideration of children as living things which is then set into the diversity of life on the planet as a whole. Scientific activities can enrich geographical investigation into physical properties, conditions for survival and the relationship between environment and human activity. Paralleling geographical questioning about themselves and the world they live in, science provides children with a complementary perspective to the question of 'Who am I?'

Observation and systematic approaches underpin the scientific exploration of the earth and the environment. Children's work on weather, rocks, soils, structure of the earth, energy and the planet's place within the universe, rely strongly on visual and physical evidence of processes and phenomena. Geographical perspectives, however, bring a subjective approach, in recognition that experiences, attitudes and feeling also shape how children interpret aspects of the world around them.

Children investigate a variety of environmental contexts at home, school or in the local area. Scientific experiments indoors can include studies of temperature (keeping warm and cool), water, materials, light, air and energy, and these can be set into wider practical contexts through reference to other places with different physical environments and lifestyles. Studies of health, hygiene, home design, clothing styles, diet, travel, transport and technology in and beyond the home in contrasting localities will gain from scientific activities and comparative approaches (see Chapter 4).

Linking with history

History and geography both help children to locate themselves in time and space. Both provide important anchor points in an era when it seems that geographical distances shrink, international boundaries come and go and histories are rewritten. Although each subject works in particular ways, adopts specific foci and interprets different sources of evidence, there are also areas of overlap.

Both subjects are concerned with understanding how to observe, interpret and make sense of evidence about inter-connected processes. Ideas such as *continuity* and *change*, *causality*, *adaptation*, *similarity* and *difference*, and *location* as well as the importance of evidence, explanation and enquiry are central to both areas of understanding. Children's developing awareness of events, evidence and interpretation in history should not be separated from geographical thinking.

Fieldwork skills assist historical enquiry. A retrievable history usually lies in the most modern of landscapes and built environments, through thinking about the site and its uses in the past. Old route ways, former land-use and place names may offer clues for children to follow. The historical record is much more apparent in some areas than others. However, even a brief local investigation combining geographical and historical approaches will help to bring the links between the past, present and (perhaps) alternative futures into closer focus. Combined subject approaches are thus ideal in a study of the local area.

Visits to historic sites may use geographical skills to question and record historical evidence. Geographical ideas may inform historical speculation on how the site and its available resources were used, or prompt considering links with other places, sources of building materials, lifestyle, technologies and the influence of ideas, peoples and goods from elsewhere. Understanding earlier life-styles and people's relationship with their surroundings, uses varied types of historical evidence and gains insights from present-day comparisons.

Working with maps should prompt historical questioning. As children use maps they find traces of past human settlement, activity and physical processes of change. Patterns of place name elements in different geographical regions prompt asking *how*, *why*, *where* and *when* earlier human activity occurred in the landscape. Plans and maps of different periods and scales help to illustrate links between physical and human processes of change. Using maps within history is comparable to using time-lines in geography, and both help children to establish spatial and temporal reference points.

Bringing reality to the past fosters historical understanding and empathy. Caricatured notions of people and life in the past are offset by drawing parallels with the present. Transferring knowledge from a historical to a contemporary situation, may also deepen the understanding of behaviour, actions and alternative outcomes. It may help to dispel notions of superiority which sometimes tinge children's views of the past. Imaginative insights into past motives, endeavour and experience may strengthen

children's understanding of people-environment relations at various levels.

Most places have a historical story to tell. The landscape, rocks and soil may hold clues about climatic conditions long ago or hint at more recent processes of change. Environmental changes might prompt enquiry into lifestyles at earlier times.

History and geography have been taught together under various labels for many years; however, where the distinctive qualities of both subjects became blurred, coherent curriculum planning tended to disappear and children's progression suffered. Developing coherent programmes which combine history and geography requires a clear grasp of each subject's essential character and an overview of the wider curriculum, so that planned activities consolidate and extend existing understanding in both areas of study.

Linking with design and technology

Design and the application of technology to many different aspects of life and human activity is so taken for granted, that questions about suitability, efficiency and overall role within society are often not adequately voiced. We live in an era in which technological innovation makes obsolescence a daily occurrence. Changes in life and work happen so fast that technology seems to become an ever more dominant force in the industrial world. It is essential that we learn to question its role so that human capacity (rather than technological determinants) dictates what and how things happen, and how societies organise and express themselves.

As the world's population becomes increasingly urbanised, fewer people live in natural environments. The vast majority live in settings which, through conscious design or

piece-meal endeavour, reflect people's unequal opportunities to provide for their basic needs. Looking at the variation within design and material well-being around the world, reveals not only the huge gulf between the rich and the poor but also – at its extreme – the human capacity to survive and ingenuity to make the most of limited resources. As the built-environment spreads across the earth's surface at unprecedented rates, it is important that children should be encouraged to reflect upon the quality and design of the world they live in.

Design and technology activities provide children with opportunities to question, evaluate and seek alternatives. Tasks draw upon many subject areas, and may support knowledge and skills across the primary curriculum. Children's geographical knowledge should include some understanding of how to plan, design, make, operate and evaluate, if they are to think and function as independent people.

Much activity within design and technology focuses on people's needs, and ways of meeting those needs with appropriate resources and particular skills. Geography provides real-world contexts within which children can develop design and technology activities. Through this the children can learn to appreciate the different opinions, preferences and value-judgements between individuals, groups and cultures. Understanding the ideas and values behind particular forms of design and technological achievement, should be accompanied by problem-solving activities where the children can design, develop and test their own tasks. This will offer insight into both the strengths and shortcomings of different designs and their relationships to specific human needs.

Indoor tasks such as designing toys, gadgets and furniture, cooking a meal or making a resealable seed packet, all lend themselves to thinking about the user's needs and situation. For example, opportunities to consider the needs of a younger class or improvements to a school site might prompt plans for sheltered sitting areas, litter bins or plant holders, and even school ponds or wildlife areas. Practical involvement in projects which address some aspect of community need and enhance the local area, clearly combine important areas of geographical understanding and competence in design and technology.

Children's respect for other life styles, skills, levels of resourcefulness and environmental adaptation usually increase as they try to work with limited resources. In their own search for effective design and appropriate resources, children can learn to appreciate an object's value to its maker and user, and understand its function in unfamiliar contexts.

Through varied practical projects and problem-solving, the skills, understanding and values of design and technology should enrich geography and foster within children sensitive and responsible attitudes towards the world around them.

Linking with art

Looking at the landscape through the eyes of an artist has a long history in many cultures and reflects the clear overlap between geography and art. Art influences landscape preferences, aesthetic judgements and cultural responses over time. Some places may be neglected, while others are so cherished that they begin to suffer. How people perceive, value and respond to the appearance of their surroundings underpins many aspects of planning, design, environmental management and improvement. The overlap between geographical concerns and creative development provides rich opportunities for cross-curricular work at primary level.

As geographers, we should use skills developed in art and design to help us to see, interpret and express our responses to different visual elements in our surroundings. By looking at them closely, we should spot shapes and the variety of patterns (intentional and accidental, natural and non-natural) and the ever-changing effects of light and shadow upon different surfaces. In the countryside, landscapes can gain meaning as outlines with curves and irregularities. These shapes can provide clues of long distant geological change and the often imperceptible processes of weathering and erosion.

Children's visual awareness of their surroundings can stimulate aesthetic and critical responses. Buildings, machinery, crops, tree-planting, bridges and other engineering feats upon skyline or landscape can elicit varied responses. In urban and rural areas, children can observe, record and evaluate many visual elements which affect the appearance and quality of their environment.

Learning to respond critically to signs and buildings, designed places and neglected spaces can help children to develop discriminatory skills and visual literacy. Skills of observation and perception underpin their ability to make informed judgements about aesthetic quality in design.

Environmental appraisal may prompt suggestions for change and, through contact with planners and designers, children can envisage, design and, in some situations, improve their surroundings. Such activities not only bring children into contact with specialists, but combine art with fieldwork skills in real situations.

Children can develop aesthetic responses to places and people through the creative use of fabric, clay, paper, card, paint and a host of other resources selected from the natural and 'made' environment. Geographical understanding and visual perception combine as children find ways to present, develop and modify ideas using varied tools and techniques, and an awareness of different traditions in art, craft and design. Direct observation, memory and imagination inform and extend children's environmental awareness and understanding.

Making and reading maps requires children to draw, design, create and use symbols, lettering and legends in effective and attractive ways. As they create maps of real and imaginary places, their awareness of colour, outline, shading and the use of space gradually develops. The visual languages of artist and cartographer extend further when children compare their own work with other examples. Historical maps offer styles of lettering and decorative features or flights of fantasy, which may stimulate practical work and imaginative thinking. Satellite images or unfamiliar views or foreign language versions of the world map, may prompt experiments in three

dimensions, collage, mixing colours or calligraphy.

Places gain meaning if they are looked at in different ways. By seeing places through the eyes of different artists at different times, insights can be made into the place, time, mind and feelings of each artist. Local studies benefit greatly if children can compare their own responses and sketches with the work of others. They can also compare different views and consider the effects of change.

The understanding of other places will benefit from a study of the art, design and craft which originated in that locality. Children can study the differences between homes, landscapes, costumes and customs and make associations with artistic works. Geographical investigations can introduce children to some of the diversity of traditional artistic forms and help them to see how the representation of ideas is influenced by time and place.

Linking with role-play and drama

Improvisation and role-play can help the children to enter the wider worlds of geographical experience. Being 'in role' helps children to develop confidence as speakers and listeners. Speaking as another character can often allow children to express geographical understanding and ideas with greater openness and less personal identification. Improvisation can offer insights into situations and foster empathy and understanding. Exploring geographical issues through drama and role-play usually requires a situation in which there are conflicting ideas about a particular course of action. Many forms of human activity and environmental geography are ideal for role-play situations since they require the children to adopt specific characters with roles,

Linking with music

Music and sound tend to be omitted from the study of place, yet they form an integral part of daily life. When studying the environment in specific localities, it is appropriate to include sound and music to develop a sense of place and an understanding of geographical diversity in the modern world.

Musical experiences offer children the ability to transcend barriers of language and attitude, and develop an awareness of other cultures and traditions at a variety of scales. This includes the opportunity to listen, sing, play and compose music. Discovering musical traditions from different peoples and places strengthens self-identity and international understanding.

Music's capacity to express ideas, thoughts and feelings offers important doorways into children's geographical understanding and imagination. Sound can also be important in fostering children's aesthetic appreciation of the world around them. It provides an alternative means through which children can envisage and understand physical processes, the enormity of some landscapes and the subtler qualities characteristic of unfamiliar environments.

Environmental concerns, social conditions and family-life may find powerful expression through musical experience. Lyrics and songs offer clues about traditional activities and contemporary issues affecting people and places. Sometimes musical experiences contribute to the distinctive identity of a particular place or community.

feelings and intentions which derive from and inform upon particular situations.

Role-play situations stimulate local investigations and may relate closely to fieldwork, interviews or meetings with specialists (including designers, planners and members of the local community). Role-play situations can also be developed in unfamiliar contexts to appreciate other viewpoints and experiences, or even in imaginary contexts which bear a resemblance to a recognisable place. In entirely fictitious settings, it is usually helpful for the children to agree on the character of their surroundings and perhaps to encourage geographical authenticity. For example, when creating a place where rivers run *uphill* and shaking trees *produce* wind, it helps for children to be aware of where their imaginary world defies real-world constraints.

Children's imaginative thinking works best if they feel confident with the material, situation or dilemma which their characters confront. Effective dramatic activity requires preparation, so that children can explore alternatives and understand other perspectives. Where the situation demands knowledge or experiences the children lack, it can lead into speculation and ill-informed judgements and action, which can be harmful both to geographical understanding and children's relationships with each other.

Apart from commercially-produced drama and role-play activities, classes can devise their own situations from photographs and broadcast programmes. News items and artefacts provide powerful and limitless starting points for geographical investigation through drama. Stories, whether improvised, retold or read, greatly enrich children's awareness of other places, peoples and predicaments (see Chapter 8).

Distant localities also gain meaning through introducing children to music and sounds associated with aspects of work, leisure, worship or festival.

Traditional musical instruments offer insights into the technical expertise and resources found within contrasting localities. Traditional instruments and music should be compared in both familiar and unfamiliar settings, so that children can recognise and appreciate common elements as well as their differences. The children should experience both traditional and contemporary music in its different forms in various places.

Unprecedented opportunities for introducing music into geography co-exist with an international music industry capable of fusing style and form. With older children, some of the processes which cause distinctive musical traditions to merge, or become submerged, within a global

sound system can be related to map-based investigation and questionnaire work on musical preferences, promotion and production.

Clearly, combining a sense of setting with the opportunity to share actively in listening, making and performing music, joins music and geography in mutually beneficial ways. Music should bring much more than background sound effects to the study of place. The music of elsewhere enables children to encounter how other people may express themselves. It provides a means to hear an insider's response to being somewhere else. Exploring geographical and environmental issues through music opens opportunities for a range of extended curricular activities and performance events. Such possibilities have many links with other areas of the curriculum and extend well beyond the framework of the geography timetable.

Linking with physical education

Physical education links with geography perhaps most obviously in the area of activities which use mapping and directional skills. Orienteering requires children to plan and follow routes. The search for signs and control points creates a real need for making or reading a map and using a compass.

Hill-walking, horse-riding, cycling and camping encourage confidence in unfamiliar settings. Competence, skill building and overall physical development are relevant to fieldwork too. These new experiences offer insights into situations encountered in stories, news reports and accounts of life in different places and periods.

Outdoor activities alert children to issues of safety in different settings. Safety depends upon sensible

behaviour and an awareness of natural and other hazards. It requires understanding personal physical needs and the importance of suitable clothing first-aid, food and water. Understanding environmental conditions confirms the importance of safety issues. The Countryside Code, conservation issues and the effect of tourism gain meaning too, as children witness the impact of some leisure activities in environmentally-sensitive areas visited during outdoor physical education.

Taking part in physical activities relates to how people live and the need for a healthy life-style. Children might compare and map, for example, sporting activities, events in the news and the origins of sports personalities. They can investigate through local surveys popular active and passive sports, the provision of sports facilities, or sport on holiday. Comparisons can be made and questions asked such as where, how and why particular sports are played elsewhere. Team or match tours could be plotted and logged in travel journals. Seasonal variations in physical conditions and personal health-care (in terms of medical precautions and diet) might link issues to a geographical sense of place. Aspects of journalism, management, advertising and site maintenance could be studied as sport-related employment.

Dance provides an alternative form in which children may express their understanding of themselves and the world around them. Movement, gesture and rhythm allow them to develop ideas in space, and capture

moods, feelings, sensations and responses to particular places and environments.

Other links between geography, dance and physical education can be imaginative and instructive too. Children might locate places associated with different dances and sports on a world map or question why certain sports are found in certain places. Alternatively, they might locate sporting events, the travels of a particular team, athlete or group of dancers. Even devising a quiz can practise locational skills as children research questions which link sports, players or events to different countries.

The influence of dance and music from other cultures upon popular taste can also invite map-related work, interviews and other links between dance and geography. From quizzes based on countries, to map work linking sport, personalities or sporting events through to a wide range of investigations, the two subjects offer interesting and imaginative opportunities for cross-curricular activities.

Linking with modern foreign languages

Children can find learning a language other than their own exciting and stimulating although, of course, where daily communication depends on becoming fluent in a language not spoken at home, many more pressures and problems may arise. This section therefore deals only with the opportunities for introducing another language dimension into the study of place.

Introducing young children to another language prepares for later linguistic development, promotes other learning skills and raises awareness about other people and places. Recognising the world's linguistic diversity is an important element within children's understanding of themselves, their own culture and their links with other countries. Children should learn that people around the world use and develop languages which may sound and look quite different, even though they may share origins and words.

Geography helps to foster positive attitudes, since it sets speakers of foreign languages, their countries and the cultures they represent into real contexts. Maps and pictures give meaning to songs, rhymes, stories and simple phrases which in turn strengthen a child's sense of place. Bilingual and multilingual children benefit from realising that their own situation is not unique and that different languages are spoken in other countries too. Places and people become more meaningful if children gain insights into the language of everyday living, and voices form part of the soundscape in any place where human activity occurs.

Language plays such a key role in the transmission of ideas and information that awareness of words, simple phrases and meaning may be part of certain geographical activities. Pictures of people and places are an obvious area of overlap, since they provide

a stimulus for language development and geographical awareness. The use of bilingual texts and stories (in translation) enriches studies on other localities, while comparative approaches may help to introduce words connected with aspects of lifestyle.

When children use street plans or maps printed in other countries, looking for recognisable and unfamiliar terms may be part of the investigative process. Travel and tourist information, passports and (depending on where the children live) signs, newspapers, menus and even instructions or labels for everyday products, may carry words in more than one language. Linguistic links with other places may exist in the words, signs and furnishings of the local environment and in everyday spoken usage too. Discussion, interviews and the use of maps, recordings,

simple phrase books and picture dictionaries can assist shopping surveys, preparing a meal from another country, or investigations into other places via language and why, when or how words travel.

Some schools may have opportunities to take geography and language links further through residential visits. The possibilities of using simple phrases and words in real situations give considerable meaning to both the place and its people, and may be explored through direct experience using maps, questionnaires, interviews and a variety of recording techniques. Exchanging children's pictures of their homes and lifestyles between schools in different countries might also be an opportunity for translating words and phrases into another language.

Reflections

Making links between subjects is a well-established practice in primary education, although it has come under criticism in recent years. This chapter has indicated how many fruitful connections occur between different subjects (which, traditionally, may not have been seen to hold much in common). In planning the primary curriculum, it is not possible to fit in all subjects at once and teachers tend to select areas of priority, whilst still striving for a broad and balanced curriculum.

For many teachers, concern about basic skills in language and number work predominates, and geography (along with other subjects) is in danger of becoming marginalised and diluted into a lack-lustre process of transmitting a medley of geographical facts. This chapter has tried to show how geography involves much more than producing children as gazetteers of geographical bric-a-brac.

There is a certain pragmatism in airing some of the links with other subjects too: geography can provide opportunities within which other areas of learning may take place.

Geography-led work may never form a very large part of the primary timetable, but it can preserve its distinctive contribution to children's understanding and development by showing that it is flexible and, where necessary, prepared to offer an extremely supportive role, even if not quite centre stage.

This chapter has not considered links with religious education, since how this area of experience is developed within the classroom is integrally connected to the specific needs of individual schools and the faith communities from which their children come within the broader context of legislative guide-lines. Ignoring the links between geography and religious education, however, would be a mistake since they both share certain important goals.

Among other reasons why children might be introduced to the religious heritage of different faiths, there are particular geographical reasons. Religious beliefs, ideas and loyalties affect aspects of the world in which children will grow up. They are a recurring theme through human history and continue to affect people's movements, actions and value systems around the globe. The influence of religion upon individuals, communities and whole societies contributes toward an understanding of self, society and the wider world. Cultural inheritance and physical landscape bear a legacy of religion which cannot be ignored.

Discussing religious beliefs helps children to form their own personal interpretations. Recognising the existence of different beliefs and values is part of a wider moral education which encourages respect and tolerance. Developing consideration for others and concern for fairness and justice, are also part of gaining insights into the lives, lifestyles and livelihoods of people in contrasting localities. Thus, religious education shares with geography a concern for fostering a better understanding between people from local to global level. Growing up in an interdependent world requires that children appreciate and respect cultural diversity, whilst also recognising that there may be underlying values and concerns which people in different cultures and societies have in common.

CHAPTER 12

The wider curriculum

Many experiences and strands of understanding interweave to produce a child's overall development at primary level. Any list of these elusive ingredients would be endless, and it is impossible to include them all as formal elements of a balanced curriculum. No-one has quite the same vision of the purpose and scope of education, so the spirit and ethos of each school will vary. However, it is helpful to distinguish key aspects of cross-curricular activity and to suggest their links with geography.

BACKGROUND

Geography for all

Various cross-curricular *dimensions* may be identified in the curriculum. They cover such issues as the appreciation of life in a multi-cultural society, special educational needs of children and equal opportunities. This means that planning for geography should endeavour to help each and every child to reach their full potential.

All children can take part in geographical exploration, although the learning outcome will be unique for each child. Geography involves the children in making discoveries about themselves, society and their surroundings. Investigations encourage children to develop skills and understanding and, at the same time, to appreciate different perspectives and experiences.

Multi-cultural society

Geography can help children form a wide view of the world. It can accommodate the tremendous ethnic, cultural and linguistic diversity of our society. It can establish the normality of difference, and through this help to dispel prejudice and ignorance. The perspectives and experiences found within other cultural settings should be seen in context and recognised and understood on their own terms.

Children should learn to tackle environmental and social issues with sensitivity, open-mindedness and informed understanding. Investigations which involve a cultural or ethnic dimension also require these skills and attitudes, so that children can explore similarities and differences in meaningful ways which positively identify and illuminate the multi- or monocultural aspects of their own locality and elsewhere.

Where ethnic communities are part of the school setting, cultural experiences and perspectives are invaluable resources for geography. Links between schools can share these opportunities and other international connections. Geography can thus help children to appreciate how dynamic processes bind places together, and weave lifestyles and landscapes into one vast interdependent and ever changing global system.

Children with learning difficulties

Geography should encourage all children to respect the different abilities of people in society. Children with physical, sensory, emotional and behavioural needs can greatly benefit from activities which enable them to explore self-identity and their sense of belonging. Varied working methods provide scope for different learning styles and help children to develop positive attitudes to

themselves and each other. First-hand investigations into the environment invite practical and imaginative responses, and can also offer answers to important questions of *who* and *where* they are.

Enquiry approaches can tailor activities to particular learning needs in flexible ways. Differentiation on fieldwork or in the classroom should enable tasks to cover the full range of ability and allow for individual progression. When group-work brings together different contributions in geographical investigations, it enables children with special educational needs to share in the success of collaborative processes and also enjoy an individual sense of achievement.

Particular difficulties arise in fieldwork for children with sensory impairment or physical disability. Finding alternative ways to give access to fieldwork experiences is desirable, but not always easy. The use of information technology, physical aids or specialist assistance may permit modified practical opportunities, and other kinds of learning, communication and skill development may be valuable outcomes. Visits to towns, farms, parks, nature reserves or wildlife sanctuaries and other locations with distinctive physical characteristics are particularly important, since they offer stimuli and scope for sensory responses.

Gifted children

No easy definition exists for a 'gifted child', but in geography a 'gifted child' would probably show an intellectual level well

above average, specific academic aptitudes, creative thinking, and a willingness to respond to intellectual and practical challenges. Investigative skills would be sophisticated, comprehensive and penetrating: they would be characterised by an ability to synthesise and interpret extensive amounts of diverse material with clarity and accuracy. Maturity of thinking and awareness of geographical ideas and issues would be apparent in problem-solving and in discussion, writing and other forms of expression.

Talented children need time for their various abilities to develop and flourish. Geographical issues, learning materials and skills in mapping, fieldwork and interpretation must meet their investigative, analytic and creative potential in challenging ways. They should recognise how geographical approaches and ideas transfer into many aspects of work at and beyond the local level.

Gender

Geography invites children to identify, investigate and interpret patterns of gender-related activity. Through direct observation and data-gathering, children can investigate patterns and trends in aspects of home-life, recreation and work. They can compare activities and opportunities, explore attitudes and images and also challenge stereotyped views. Children should have first-hand experience of different working environments and meet people participating in occupations at different levels. In making sense of other places and other lifestyles, equality of opportunity and other cultural conventions should be set within the broader social and physical environment.

All children should have the opportunity to take a full part in investigations. They should

The A426 By Pass Plan

For	Against
• Less dangerous for local people	• Will mean knocking down ho...
• No lorries in High street	• Noisi... for
• Quieter	• Pollutio...
• No damage to old buildings	• Dangero...
	• Spoils countr...

Cross-curricular themes

Among many themes which pervade the whole curriculum, five have become pre-eminent, notably:
• economic and industrial understanding;
• environmental education;
• health education;
• citizenship;
• careers education and guidance.
They represent key areas of understanding and experience in the modern curriculum and, in varying ways, contribute to how children understand and participate in the world around them.

each experience being both leader and team member in group-work, and become competent with handling equipment in the classroom and elsewhere. They should encounter situations where they can see geographical competence and expertise extending into working opportunities for both men and women in and beyond the local area.

Transferable skills

In the primary school, children develop many core skills which are transferable across the whole curriculum. These skills include: communication, numeracy, problem-solving and the use of information technology.

Fostering personal and social skills is integral to the children's preparation for adult life. Geography should encourage the development of these skills to help the children become independent, responsive and responsible

citizens with value systems which inform their thoughts, actions and attitudes towards other people, living things and their surroundings.

Communicating ideas through image, word, map, plan, model, number and diagram is an integral element of geography. Enquiry-based learning involves talking, listening, reading and writing in various forms, for different purposes, with different audiences and in response to or assisted by different media. Geography requires numeracy as children gather, sort and interrogate data, make calculations, map, plan, design or construct and otherwise apply numerical skills.

Problem-solving occurs within real or imaginary contexts. It helps the children to work on their own, in groups or with adults in varied situations. Open-ended tasks provide children with a conscious understanding of the decision-making process. Varied geographical approaches, issues and sources of data should thus offer opportunities for children to become competent, confident and creative in the classroom and later life.

Economic and industrial understanding

Children form a critical mass within society and the economy. When societies meet their basic needs and provide support for their development, investment is being made for the future. Children's age of entry into the world of work has varied through time and geographical space, but their entry into the economy starts even before they are born! Young children soon become consumers as adults respond variously to their needs, wishes and increasing ability to influence economic decisions, options and the use of resources. Finding ways to bring together the young child's disparate personal economic experiences and encounters with the world of work, lies at the core of economic and industrial understanding.

Geography has the potential to equip children with knowledge, skills, understanding and attitudes relevant to their present and future lives. It introduces diverse real-world contexts within which economic awareness may develop. Everyday situations should alert children to the range of resources, their value and availability, and also the importance of efficient resource management. Comparisons reveal how resource opportunities vary between individuals, groups and societies and have major implications for lifestyle, livelihood and landscape.

Economic understanding requires that children should appreciate some of the differences between *want* and *need*. The basic need for food, clothing, shelter and rest is central to human existence and underlies geographical comparisons of lifestyles. Children should learn that even basic human needs are not available for all, and that need has different meanings to different people in different times and places. The media plays a critical role in developing children's awareness of different economic experiences by portraying images of want and need.

Fieldwork offers direct experiences of places where children may meet adults who have varied kinds of employment and skills. Children should appreciate how different people's work contributes to the character of their surroundings and their own lives. Investigating where people live and work might lead children to collect, analyse and interpret information about local economic activity. Visits to shops, markets, travel centres and a range of public and private services will foster economic awareness.

Children can also explore how technology, consumer decisions and economic choices affect the quality of their environment, their own lifestyles and also the lives, work and surroundings of other people too. The children can see the environmental consequences of personal decisions, preferences and actions at a local and more distant level through observation and practical activities.

Environmental education

Environmental awareness is central to children's understanding of themselves and the outer world. Children should have an entitlement to learning *about* their surroundings and have opportunities to explore, work and play *in* different environments: from these experiences should come a genuine and lasting appreciation *for* the world and its diversity.

Developing knowledge, understanding, concern and respect for the environment should span all areas of the curriculum. The children should recognise that individual and collective responsibility is essential for

environmental quality, material and personal well-being and the overall survival of an increasingly fragile planet.

Basic environmental knowledge and understanding comes from geographical concern for a range of physical, human and environmental issues. Areas of geographical interest which have particular significance within environmental education include resources, environments under threat, and environmental management and protection.

Environmental fieldwork offers children direct experiences in practical learning situations where considerable personal, social and intellectual development may occur. However, enquiry-based activities should be such an integral element of children's geographical

experiences that the use of the environment as an outdoor classroom is not restricted to environmental education.

Geography's concern for people-place relationships cannot help but consider attitudes and values embedded in ideas, action and decisions affecting the people and environments of the planet. Practical activities, problem-solving and fieldwork involve children in collaborative and independent ways of working which encourage balanced views and interpretations. Through personal involvement and action, children can recognise wider inter-connections between people, places and processes of environmental change around the globe.

Health education

Geography can alert children to many issues of health and safety in the world around them. Personal care and

cleanliness in and beyond the home might be part of looking at lifestyles in contrasting settings. Healthy eating habits, hygiene, dental care and caring for themselves, other people and living creatures as well as their surroundings, raise children's sense of personal responsibility.

Comparing different lifestyles in contrasting localities helps children to understand the effects of limited opportunities to medical help and basic health-care, food and clean drinking water. Recording daily water consumption, and carrying or filtering water will encourage the children's awareness of different health issues. Water, pollution and the weather are variables which affect the quality of life everywhere. Surveys in the local area identify such aspects as health-care provision, how people travel from place to place and participation in physical recreation. Visits from school health-workers or visits to a clinic or hospital, offer insights into different types of work as well as health education.

Safety issues are essential considerations in any fieldwork visit. Children need to be aware of the potential hazards in certain places and in using some equipment. The permanent or seasonal risks which face people working in different environments should be identified when children carry out interviews and surveys on farms, ports, railway or power stations, construction or industrial sites and other outdoor or underground sites.

Dangers and health risks in the local environment, home and school can also be discussed although some

require sensitive handling where cultural and religious issues are concerned just like other investigations into behaviour, habits and belief. Finally, geography can also contribute to health education through exploring house design, building regulations and design codes, environmental preference surveys or different types of practical site improvement project.

Citizenship

Children gradually begin to recognise in primary school how their own lives connect with many other people. They begin to see how these people, in turn, are each part of a family, a wider community, and how this community is part of society. Making sense of how all these three elements are linked across distance and time by a web of roles, relationships, responsibilities, duties and rights, clearly goes far beyond primary school, but this is where much of the discovery process starts.

Geography's concern about people and places helps children to see how they relate to others (both near and far) within many aspects of their daily lives. These discoveries foster a clearer sense of belonging and identify. Links between people at different scales, gain meaning through familiarity with maps, globes and atlases. Investigations enable children to question and to piece together patterns of similarity, diversity and interdependence in their own surroundings and elsewhere.

Geography helps children to locate themselves and their family in space. Local studies reveal how family life is part of

a wider community in which decisions, actions, duties and rights influence how people relate to each other, their surroundings and farther afield. The children might talk with people involved in different parts of the local community. Visitors, interviews and questionnaire surveys can identify how opinions vary, decisions are made, why problems occur and how needs are best met. Surveys of everyday concerns in familiar contexts can reveal how attitudes, actions and needs of individuals, groups and whole communities may have distant causes and far-reaching consequences.

Through geography, children can explore what makes their community distinctive, how and why it works in particular ways, and how it is part of a wider multi-cultural society in which there are diverse ethnic groups, languages, beliefs and human experiences. Home and school

are important anchor points to establish within the wider setting: they may provide scope for exploring continuity and change and patterns of diversity.

School may be an important context for children to explore why and how people behave in particular ways, and to understand their own responsibilities and rights. Through group work and activities which bring different together age-groups, geography can encourage children to develop open and positive attitudes towards themselves, each other and their surroundings. From this basis, more complex aspects of society can be introduced. Geography therefore assists citizenship by offering a framework within which knowledge, belief and values derive from and extend first-hand experience.

Careers education and guidance

Children's early awareness of work activities which involve people in and beyond the home begin before coming to school, through animals, uniforms and vehicles associated with different kinds of work. Play often imitates adult working-life and is influenced through observation, visits, television and stories. Learning activities frequently practise skills required in particular kinds of work, such as counting coins, constructing models, writing, drawing, solving problems and communicating with other people.

Geography encourages the awareness of work activities through introducing situations in school, the local area and further afield (visits, visitors, surveys, stories, simulations, role-play activities and videos). These activities help the children to develop a vocabulary of work-related words, to consider different jobs within particular kinds of work and to identify what they like most or least. Changes in work opportunities relate to why people move into or away from places and how change occurs. Geographical questioning about work might start from observable local evidence and build up a database for varied forms of analysis.

Any consideration of work introduces children to the importance of working responsibly in and away from the classroom. On visits to places of employment, children recognise the importance of working effectively in practical situations, the need to be able to make decisions, act with initiative and evaluate their own work. The importance of being punctual and efficient is clearly demonstrated by meeting people in unfamiliar working contexts.

Insights into other peoples' work broadens children's experiences and gives meaning to lifestyles and working situations found elsewhere. Types of work involving journeys by road, rail, air or other forms of transport could also be compared in different countries (using maps to consider distances, route-planning and travelling conditions). Environmental issues such as seasonal change, traffic, noise, pollution congestion, energy consumption, and distance between home and work, link this cross-curricular theme with other geographical topics.

Reflections

*The distinctive perspective of the geographer must not be lost amid the subject's connections with cross-curricular elements. Geography, for all its changes in and beyond primary level, still asks the question **where**? in its concern about space. Geographical investigations discover where things happen, where human activities occur and how places, people and processes interrelate at different scales. Location influences the ideas, actions and experience of individuals, groups and whole societies. Indeed, it affects how we each regard and respond to our surroundings and the wider world. Through geographical activity, children should become equipped to discover places for themselves and the means to participate positively in the world around them.*

CHAPTER 13

Planning

Planning a curriculum is rather like putting together a very complicated puzzle. Individual subjects are combined in different ways to form a broad and balanced curriculum. However, the puzzle is assembled in such a way that once completed other strands can be seen running through it as cross-curricular themes.

Planning the curriculum requires organisation and clarity at every level. Most schools have a planning structure in which the head teacher, subject coordinator and staff see how the curriculum pieces join together at various scales. The head teacher may be more concerned with the overview of the curriculum, but the staff play an equally important role in understanding its detailed application.

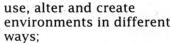

BACKGROUND

Planning with a purpose

In planning for geographical education in the primary school it is important that we understand what 'geography' is all about. In England, the National Curriculum Council defines geography as being concerned with 'the study of places, the human and physical processes which shape them and the people who live in them'. Geography should thus help children to 'make sense of their surroundings and the wider world'. The National Curriculum Council also lists a number of attainment targets and programmes of study which should be included in the teaching of geography.

A number of broad aims can be identified which provide a basis for children's geographical learning experiences. A study of geography should help children to:

• develop a lasting appreciation of their surroundings and the diversity of physical and human conditions on the Earth's surface;
• gain a sense of place and a locational framework that will support other geographical experiences and learning;
• recognise how places and people are interdependent in a rapidly changing world;
• appreciate the relationship between environment and human activities, and the need for responsible action and attitudes towards the Earth and its peoples;
• realise that people perceive, use, alter and create environments in different ways;
• begin to develop informed responses to issues of conflicting interest, environmental quality and social well-being;
• realise that geographical issues and evidence may be interpreted in different ways;
• apply a variety of investigative approaches and techniques;
• develop personal responsibility for how they learn on their own and interact with others.

The study of geography should help children to develop a sense of personal identity and an awareness of the world as a whole. This should foster a sense of humanity and environmental responsibility and thus contribute to the children's own development as sensitive, thoughtful and independent people.

Geography for the whole school

Developing a policy for geography requires that the school reaches broad agreement on four interrelated aspects of curriculum planning:
• the curriculum;
• teaching and learning;
• resources;
• management.

1. The curriculum
The school should reach agreement on what is to be

taught and how effectively it is to be learned. Policy statements might include information on:
• geographical content (skills, places and themes);
• contexts for learning;
• continuity and progression;
• differentiation;
• assessment and recording;
• planning guidelines for schemes of work.

2. Teaching and learning

The school should reach agreement on how the curriculum is delivered and received. Policy statements might include information on:
• enquiry and issue-based approaches;
• fieldwork;
• learning experiences;
• teaching and learning styles;
• cross-curricular subjects, skills, dimensions and themes;
• managing learning and recording;
• classroom organisation (space and group size);
• role and contribution of teachers, parents and other adults.

3. Resources

The school should reach agreement on what is used to help the geography curriculum. Policy statements might include information on:
• teaching materials and equipment;
• printed text and visual resources;
• geographical artefacts;
• information technology;
• resource organisation;
• fieldwork;
• visits and off-site opportunities;
• community and work-place contacts;
• visitors and supporting adults;
• resource bases and outside agencies;

• display areas;
• use of school site.

4. Management

The school should reach agreement on the procedures for organising curriculum, teaching and learning and resources. Policy statements might include information on:
• coordination and leadership;
• classroom procedures;
• discipline, health and safety;
• curriculum implementation;
• staff development;
• evaluation and review;
• community and environmental links;
• school links and exchanges;
• liaison with feeder schools.

These aspects of curriculum planning should offer a basis for an agreed geography policy. They should help geography to find a purposeful place within the school and, like all aspects of curriculum planning, should periodically come under review.

An action plan for geography

After developing a policy for geography, the next planning step is to make a school development plan. This plan should identify how the statements of principle and policy translate into reality. Ideally, it should prioritise areas of need and curriculum change in the short, medium and long term. It should also be flexible, adaptable and helpful in planning for the needs of all children and teachers in the school.

In order to keep track of geography in overall curriculum thinking the school needs a curriculum leader or coordinator. The geography coordinator can then consult with the head teacher and share the planning issues with other staff. Early in the planning process, the geography coordinator should review the existing provision for geography. The findings of this stocktaking process should become a basis for subsequent planning. The geography coordinator could compile information by asking the following questions:
• What is the range of areas, themes and places (local, national, international, global)?

• Which geographical skills are practised (mapping, graphicacy, enquiry, problem-solving, data-handling)?
• Is there evidence of continuity and progression (introduction, practice, extension and application of skills, ideas and understanding in geographical learning)?
• Is there any fieldwork (school site, immediate vicinity, local area, further afield)?
• Are any visits and visitors associated with geography (local walks, trails, half-day or longer outings for single subject or cross-curricular activities; relations, teachers from elsewhere, community leaders, specialists in public, private and voluntary sector)?
• What resources are available in school, locally and within travelling distance (quantity, quality, availability, suitability, relevance)?

• What relevant contacts exist locally and further afield (community, school, family and personal links; historical, political, cultural, environmental, business and industrial links)?
• What geographical strengths may exist in the school, its members and its setting (travel and work experiences, contacts, artefacts, resources, visitors, other languages)?
• What short, medium and long term constraints exist (appropriate resources, mixed-ability and year groups, space, fieldwork, expertise, staffing and teaching support)?
• What corresponds with the National Curriculum requirements (in existing geography or other curriculum areas)?
• How much time is available for geography (per week, term, year or over each Key Stage)?
• Where does geography appear in the timetable (single subject, combined and integrated approaches)?

This stocktaking process will identify the school's geographical needs and opportunities. It should identify the desirable goals or outcomes for each, some or every child and relate geography to wider aims for educational, personal and social development.

Timetabling geography

In most primary schools, timetables should give geography the equivalent of one afternoon per week. Tight time management means that teachers need to identify a clear focus, keep learning goals and outcomes in mind, and prioritise how time can be best spend in different activities. Geography can be included in the primary curriculum in various ways:
• in an integrated topic;
• in a combined-subject topic;
• in a geography-led topic;
• as a discrete subject.

Integrated topic

Geography can be combined with other curriculum areas in an integrated topic. This approach is familiar to primary school teachers and is thought to help children connect areas of learning with areas of experience. It also spreads the demand for resources. However, the drawbacks are that time allocation is spread thinly between subjects, progression is sometimes difficult to ascertain and the concepts introduced are over-ambitious.

Combined-subject topic

Geography can be included as part of a combined-subject topic. This offers the children links between learning experiences, but prioritises

where the learning emphasis is placed and how the time is spent. However, the drawbacks are that this blurs and creates divisions between subjects in arbitrary ways and may restrict open-ended enquiries and problem-solving approaches.

Geography at the centre

Geography can be put at the centre of the learning focus, drawing upon other curricular areas for support. In this case, geography is given a distinctive role and additional time is spent on studying the subject. This may lose some of the rich diversity of cross-curricular approaches, but gives geography a clear identity.

Geography as a discrete subject

A single subject focus treats geography as a discrete subject with a clear slot in the timetable. This allows geographical activity the maximum amount of time with specific resources. However, this approach is more associated with secondary education and is not widespread in initial primary teacher education. It requires the maximum of resources and confines teaching to an inflexible amount of time.

Developing a curriculum plan

Figure 1 illustrates different approaches to geography depending on the availability of time. Although many schools plan geography as part of their *topic* slot on the time-table, the term *theme* (rather than topic) is used to indicate blocks of time and thus avoids emphasising any single approach to teaching geography.

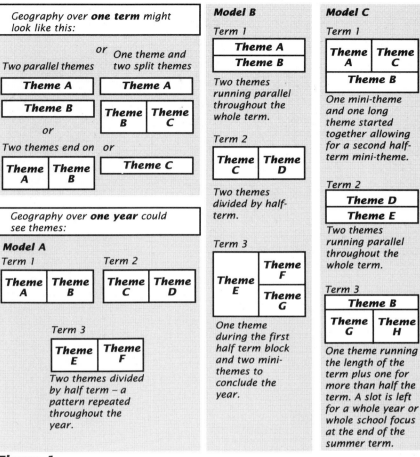

Patterns of planning

*Geography over **one term** might look like this:*

Two parallel themes or *One theme and two split themes*

Theme A

Theme B

or

Theme A

| Theme B | Theme C |

Two themes end on or

| Theme A | Theme B |

Theme C

*Geography over **one year** could see themes:*

Model A

Term 1

| Theme A | Theme B |

Term 2

| Theme C | Theme D |

Term 3

| Theme E | Theme F |

Two themes divided by half term – a pattern repeated throughout the year.

Model B

Term 1

Theme A

Theme B

Two themes running parallel throughout the whole term.

Term 2

| Theme C | Theme D |

Two themes divided by half-term.

Term 3

| Theme E | Theme F / Theme G |

One theme during the first half term block and two mini-themes to conclude the year.

Model C

Term 1

| Theme A | Theme C |

Theme B

One mini-theme and one long theme started together allowing for a second half-term mini-theme.

Term 2

Theme D

Theme E

Two themes running parallel throughout the whole term.

Term 3

Theme B

| Theme G | Theme H |

One theme running the length of the term plus one for more than half the term. A slot is left for a whole year or whole school focus at the end of the summer term.

Figure 1

Themes may split available time into parallel units, successive units, or teachers may keep the slot as a single block of time. This depends on how teachers wish to develop their themes, which may span half a term or a whole term (or even longer if they have internal changes of focus). Running two quite separate themes concurrently, is simpler than trying to prevent similar themes from merging. Careful planning can introduce appropriate links with other subjects.

Alternatively, teachers may develop mini-themes which last for one week or more. These can be particularly useful ways of raising awareness of specific issues and aspects of geography. The geography plan should allow for teachers to develop a variety of long and short themes as appropriate.

Geography across one or both Key Stages should adopt a pattern of planning over the years which balances breadth *between* themes and depth *within* individual themes, according to the children's intellectual development and their awareness of the world.

By adopting a variety of approaches, the children should be able to combine breadth with more sharply-focused work. Other whole school options may exist too: a half-term narrow focus on

geography, for instance, might involve children working on different aspects which are all brought together as the study progresses.

Opportunities which require older children working with or on behalf of younger children, can bring not only a real-world dimension to a practical problem-solving issue, but also foster positive attitudes between year groups which extend into other aspects of school life. Working together offers teachers and children scope for trying and sharing new ideas. Combining geography with a cross-curricular theme might also be a springboard for a stimulating half-term focus.

There should also be space for other geographical learning experiences. Informal discussion occasioned by news, holidays, events, visits or visitors, broadcast programmes, stories, games and the arrival of the unexpected, also foster children's wider geographical understanding and awareness. Geography is enriched by these informal references and should make appropriate links, which means building flexibility into the timetable and ensuring that space for topical issues remains in the curriculum plan. A rolling programme for geography over a term or year (or Key Stage) could reserve periods of time for non-specified (at the time of planning) timetabled activities. This has considerable educational merits for a class, year group or whole school, although implications for the wider curriculum depend on the time and numbers involved.

Themes with a shifting focus

Changing from an integrated to a more narrowly-defined curriculum plan seems less daunting if a chosen theme has a shifting focus. This means that the emphasis changes as the study continues. For instance, a geography-led theme on a locality in the developing world, might shift to a focus on design and technology as the children develop practical ideas and problem-solving activities. This might conclude the chosen theme or, if it warranted further investigation, the focus might change to another subject such as science. In this way, detailed work in two or more subjects could be matched by exploring connections to other areas.

It does not matter whether a chosen theme starts or moves to its focus in geography, as this will depend on the nature of work being planned. For instance, a theme on 'Ancient Greece' might start with holiday travel and modern tourism, then change to an emphasis on science, mathematics or design and technology through work on structures and materials, and then lead on to history. In this way clues in the modern landscape become a catalyst for solving practical problems and exploring people and society in the past. Conversely, a theme on 'Invaders and Settlers' might start from a strong history focus, lead on to language-related activities, and use place name evidence and fieldwork to combine a historical presence with geographical reality.

A linear planning model can therefore bring together subjects and draw upon other curriculum areas, as appropriate. Clearly, this example of planning has value, although it might not be advisable to run two themes with changing emphasis at the same time.

Schemes of work

Schemes of work are outline plans; sometimes they are used to describe plans which span an entire Key Stage, more usually they deal with detailed planning over a series of sessions. They should have a clear statement of intent about the work and how it links with the rest of the curriculum. A series of key questions can focus attention on the intended outcome, and should underpin the choice and sequencing of geographical activities (which should involve children in a variety of learning styles). The allocation of time for each activity (or unit of work) and details of the resources and organisation should be noted. Teachers might build in opportunities for assessment and record-keeping at this stage too.

Schemes of work should indicate activities for children with different abilities. Clear differentiation *between* and *within* tasks is essential. Prior planning can usefully indicate where and how assessment, continuity and progression should occur. Plans might identify relevant Attainment Targets in geography and other subjects too. In short, the scheme of work provides a framework into which the detailed planning of individual lessons may be slotted. It should be a working document and should indicate where the

changes occurred. In this way, the scheme can be a summary class record of geography work undertaken and, if saved, a resource for other teachers.

Mixed ages and abilities

In planning geography for children of mixed ages and abilities, teachers must try to accommodate the differences in understanding, skill acquisition, and personal interests and development. This is easier if the geography curriculum shows a clear framework for skill development (for example, using the programmes of study and statements of attainment). Developing activities appropriate to different levels of understanding and ability requires extensive resourcing and builds from your experience of the geography curriculum.

Many activities in this book have included extension suggestions which offer

different forms of differentiation. Sometimes, the *tasks* may differ, and require separate resources and different ways of working. Sometimes the *outcome* is different, as children will be involved in the same task but operating at different levels of achievement. At times, variations upon a broadly similar activity produce a *structured sequence* of tasks.

Mixed-ability classes often tackle geographical activities through group work, but this is sometimes difficult and may require support staff. Where classes have mixed Key Stages, looking for the recurring strands within the statements of attainment, attainment targets and programmes of study should help to identify the sequence of development across the levels. Revisiting part of the Programme of Study seems unavoidable but, wherever this is likely to

happen, efficient record-keeping should allow teachers to build positively on earlier experience. When ideas are met more than once the learning process can be one of reinforcement rather than repetition. Differentiation can help older children to gain something new from a second encounter.

Geography can sometimes turn difficulties to its advantage. Possibilities for children helping each other, or learning from their peers and elders, play an important role in enquiry and problem-solving activities. Older children might develop practical environment-based activities with younger children in mind: their audience provides a real-world context for the development of trails, model layouts, board games, floor puzzles, map-making and so forth. Far from being in a passive role, young children can offer opinions, preferences, and require considerable input from the older children.

Planning for children with special learning difficulties

Planning geography for children with special learning difficulties requires clearly differentiated tasks, appropriate to individual needs and abilities. The Attainment Targets and Programmes of Study use some command terms (such as *explain*, *identify* or *describe*) which may be based on observation, coordination or communication. Such terms may be beyond the experiences of children dependent upon signing and symbol vocabularies, and inappropriate for children with difficulties in communication, vision, mobility or coordination. These requirements need to be translated into simpler situations, so that children with moderate or severe learning difficulties can participate.

Careful preparation helps to make activities more explicit, so that children know what they are to do and, how to set about doing it; and reinforces how their work forms part of a wider understanding about themselves and the world around them. A clear focus and simple instructions can help the children to work in and beyond the classroom.

The school environment and immediate vicinity provide an accessible and doorstep resource which can be re-visited during investigative work. Facilities and support staff may be more flexibly deployed on-site than in other locations. Exploring the school environment together is particularly important for these children, since school may be one of the few experiences they can share when they come from widespread homes and have highly individual needs.

Practical activities bring geographical awareness and foster competence in many everyday situations. Site-work on litter, minibeasts, weather, improvements in the grounds or developing a school garden, wildlife area or raised plant holders, fosters environmental awareness, stimulates interests and builds self-confidence in outdoor situations. Wherever possible, children should learn by doing and direct involvement. Interviews, surveys, questions and scavenger hunts for clues around the school provide children with their own set of data which they might record, classify, sort and interpret in different ways. Discoveries

about the school site, community and how it is organised, offer children insights into a microcosm of wider society and people-place relationships.

Play apparatus can be useful in developing geographical awareness. Construction toys, model layouts and playhouses encourage children to explore spatial relationships, and to stimulate children's use and understanding of geographical vocabulary. Games based on pairing cards, throwing dice, collecting card sets, or following instructions to travel around a board, may encourage environmental awareness while also assisting the development of language, memory and social skills.

Working with three-dimensional maps, rock and mineral specimens, models and artefacts, will stimulate the children's tactile responses and this may help their understanding in fieldwork. Sensory approaches may be developed through using play apparatus to construct mazes or obstacle courses. Orientation skills based on the senses might help the children to follow trails themselves or to devise them for younger children. Large-scale floor mats, giant maps or place puzzles, and inflatable or soft-filled globes, can familiarise children with the wider world. Approaches which use the senses through art, music and movement also create greater awareness of the world beyond.

Much planning for children without visual impairment will involve activities based on observation. Street-based work, matching observable evidence to photographs (or video) encourages fieldwork skills. It may include data collection and interpretation on colours, patterns, shapes, sounds, smells, and likes and dislikes about the local area. The visual nature of geography lends itself to matching activities of many kinds and the opportunities for piecing together words, pictures, symbols and artefacts are considerable. Matching sounds to specific locations within a room, or following a soundtrail blind-folded, can foster directional understanding. Sounds associated with different setting, can introduce children to a sense of place.

Planning for children with special learning needs requires matching tasks to specific needs through cross-curricular approaches. A number of the activities suggested in other chapters may have relevance after some modification. Chapter 1 offers some possibilities which may be of particular relevance, although their intellectual level needs to be balanced against the suitability for children of different physical, emotional and social maturities.

The use of information technology offers important opportunities for children with poor coordination and limited language skills (see Chapter 10). Many of these children may not be able to tackle much above the first level of achievement, but through enthusiastic and effective planning for clearly differentiated tasks, based on varied learning approaches, their entitlement to geography can be met in meaningful and enjoyable ways.

Planning for fieldwork

Work outside the classroom is part of the children's geographical entitlement. Outdoor geography should stimulate spatial and environmental awareness at every stage, and enable children to view familiar and less familiar places with new levels of appreciation and insight. Geography encourages children to develop understanding about contrasting environments: fieldwork and visits help to formalise and consolidate pre-school learning.

Sadly, as many children are able to travel further and further afield, they know less and less about where they live. Providing fieldwork opportunities through school is becoming increasingly important, particularly as modern risks reduce the children's personal safety, compromise independent play and restrict unsupervised exploration. Practical activities and first-hand experience in the local area can help to develop children's geographical awareness and provide a firm basis for more sophisticated approaches.

Fieldwork should develop a range of approaches and techniques within contrasting environments at different scales and distances from school. Places and working methods may be re-visited, but children should constantly extend their skills in observation, classification, recording and explanation, and develop a wider vocabulary and greater environmental awareness.

It is useful to develop a school policy which sets out the fieldwork opportunities to be encountered during a child's time in school. The Attainment Targets and Programme of Study identify working methods and concepts suitable for different levels of achievement. Children's changing awareness, understanding and investigative skill should be matched against the potential of accessible sites. Sequencing fieldwork experiences requires making an appraisal of the opportunities available in particular places for different age-groups. This review will help to identify where, when and how frequently the children should experience different fieldwork activities which build on and extend prior learning.

Reflections

Planning for geography will take time, effort and money. It is necessary to prioritise where action needs to take place and acknowledge that resources and expertise can only develop gradually. The school buildings, grounds and community provide a more immediate resource suitable for different forms of investigation at any age. The unique and personal character of school-generated data also makes sharing material between schools an enjoyable and highly motivating process for children.

Developing resources for geography can be made easier if widened to include colleagues, parents and friends. Imaginative resource planning should include identifying contacts, interest points in the locality, fieldwork and work-place opportunities. Contacts should be set up with resources bases such as the planning department, tourist centres, local studies and archives. A range of resources may be available from development agencies and other organisations within the public, private and voluntary sector. Collections of pictures, postcards, brochures, packets and labels, coins, stamps, objects, and ephemera (such as tickets, timetables and till receipts) could all prompt geographical enquiry.

Contacts with other schools might share fieldwork possibilities. Cooperation might also ease problems of storage and cost. Finding ways to overcome professional isolation is important: sharing ideas, comparing curriculum programming, exchanging schemes of work and pooling resources for specific themes and places, could greatly enrich primary teaching and learning. Above all, planning must ensure that suitable amounts of time are identified in the school year for these developments to take place. Finding a place for geography in the primary curriculum requires that it be allotted realistic amounts of the timetable.

CHAPTER 14

Assessment

Assessment and recording children's work are part of daily classroom life. No effective learning can take place without teachers helping children through the interrelated processes of observing, recording and keeping work under review. Monitoring children's activities indicates their potential, achievements and areas for improvement. This continuous process should operate at a range of scales throughout each day, week, term and year.

Assessment is therefore nothing new and must be kept strictly in perspective. It should be a flexible tool and must be responsive to the children's and teacher's situation. It should be integral to any curriculum plan through the primary school. Above all, assessment strategies should be meaningful, manageable and minimal in the disruption of children's learning.

BACKGROUND

Planning for assessment

Any school's ultimate goal is to have a purposeful, effective and enjoyable curriculum. Greater emphasis on planning for structured progression inevitably brings calls to formalise the assessment process and to make criteria used in evaluation more explicit. Assessment has always been, and should remain, a matter for professional judgement. In the past, much has tended to be informal, intuitive and usually directly linked to the normal course of geographical activities. Greater openness on the use of assessment criteria, and clearer recognition of children's achievements and attainments, should enhance rather than impede teaching and learning in geography.

We must constantly ask ourselves what assessment is for. There is little point in devising systems which constrain and restrict the character of geographical investigation and children's learning. Questioning *what*, *why* and *how* to assess should inform planning, and help teachers to avoid atomising the curriculum into a series of fragments carrying a tick or a cross. This latter approach only wastes time, generates unwieldy amounts of information and disrupts geographical learning. At best it remains a crude indicator of children's achievement. Usually, this approach is too time-consuming to compile and decode diagnostic planning.

Formal evaluation does not require the constant assessment of everything. However, it does require that the teacher should be clear about the learning objectives of each geographical activity.

Strategies in assessment

Teachers should use any National Curriculum requirement as a guide to what, why and how they might plan. For example, Attainment Targets and Programmes of Study can be points of reference against which plans for schemes of work over a term, year or Key Stage may be set. They will help to ensure balance and breadth in the coverage of different areas of geographical understanding, skills and attitudes. They can be seen as potential indicators of geographical understanding at different stages in a child's development, but they should not become the sole determinants of the geography curriculum.

Any attempt to define criteria for assessment faces a number of problems. Geographical experiences are too multi-faceted to fit easily into little boxes, and prescriptive systems of assessment can leave things out. Geography enables all sorts of learning to occur and unexpected discoveries deserve a place in the recording of children's progression. It is important that any assessment strategy should not dilute the value, meaning and enjoyment of geography.

Assessment should draw upon a wide range of evidence: some activities leave a record in written, artistic or graphical form; others leave no record, but may reflect children's understanding in discussion, improvisation, data-handling, problem-solving and so on. Assessment must consider *how* and *why* as well as *what* children learn. The regular effective observation of children's learning is both diagnostic and formative. It can link observations and responses to the child's previous achievements but it can also involve the child directly or be part of a wider class evaluation. Achievements in different contexts in and beyond the classroom can be mentally noted or recorded in photographs or on video. Sound recordings can yield valuable oral evidence, but they require considerable time for playing back.

Some samples of children's work can be kept as permanent evidence for assessment. Examples should show the landmarks and stages of achievement in the child's progress. Children can help to select representative material and comment upon it in relation to previous or future work. It can be filed for future reference or taken home. Wherever possible, the samples of children's work should reflect the diversity of their geographical learning, but practical limits on storage will inevitably limit the selection.

Planning for assessment means being clear about the particular skills, concepts and attitudes in different activities.

There are four different kinds of assessment evidence within which various tasks can be grouped (see Figure 1). From the start, children must be encouraged to evaluate and identify their own strengths and achievements as well as opportunities for improvement. As children learn to recognise quality in their own work and that of others, their growing critical awareness brings greater self-reliance. This in turn encourages the children to appraise their own efforts with even greater rigour and helps to wean them from being so narrowly dependent on teacher evaluation. Once children understand *why* they are working in a particular way, this not only informs them about *what* they are doing, but also about *how* the work should be done. Greater personal responsibility can be fostered by the variety of situations in which geography takes place:
• during fieldwork: by taking responsibility for equipment,

Written evidence:	Descriptions, reports, notes, letters, diaries and logs, stories, poems, news reports, advertisements, brochures, questionnaires, site survey sheets, posters, trail guides, travel itineraries and route plans, quiz questions, word searches, cloze procedures, multiple-choice questions, short answer questions, worksheets, displays and exhibitions, and paper and pencil tests.
Graphical evidence:	Maps and plans, drawings, diagrams, place time-lines, computer print-outs, photographs, and atlas scavenger hunts.
Oral evidence:	Discussion, interviews, questioning, debates, role play and improvisation, balloon debates, presentations, tape-slide sequences, video recording, tape recording, mini-conferences, word association games, brainstorming, and sequencing.
Other forms of evidence:	Design briefs, models, artefacts, board games, floor games, card games, using programmable toys, practical investigations using equipment, and looking into a camera.

Figure 1

data collection and recording, personal and collective safety, and their own behaviour;
• in group-work and problem-solving activities: when working with others, seeking alternative strategies and in questioning processes;

• in evaluating activities afterwards: by the effectiveness of their working methods, their use of resources, their sharing of equipment, data and tasks, their patterns of interpretation and their means of presentation.

Children should be encouraged to judge for themselves when they think work is complete. Checking work on their own or with a partner (prior to seeking the teacher's confirmation of its completion and acceptability) focuses attention on the task in hand, encourages discriminatory skills and encourages children to adopt higher standards. The children can appraise their own and each other's written activities, number-work and their use of maps, plans and photographs in different practical contexts as part of wider evaluation processes.

Children can become more motivated once assessment is opened out to them. The evaluation criteria should be familiar to them so that they can understand and apply it to their geographical work, and terms need to be simple and specific as a result. Confidence in recognising their own achievement not only fosters self-esteem, but is a springboard for setting new goals.

Self-evaluation sheets for geography

Self-evaluation should take place when each geography theme is complete. By using photocopiable recording sheets, evaluations could be shared or filed along with examples of completed work. These could be working documents to promote discussion or exist as more personal statements of hopes and intentions.

Global aims

Children should have the opportunity to reflect upon geography at the end of a theme or topic. A set of labels (see photocopiable page 191) showing children's responses to questions regarding learning successes, hopes and intentions, areas of interest or shortcomings to overcome, could be superimposed on different continents on a blank outline map of the world. Changing the position of the labels (or creating imaginary islands) would avoid any negative links with particular continents. Alternatively, this could become a statement of goals and concerns which derive or start from a longer focus on environmental geography.

Theme sheets

Filling in a recording sheet for individual topics or themes using words or pictures provides a record of work and helps the children to become aware of their own learning. Teachers may design their own sheet for each theme or use a general purpose sheet for all geography topics – see photocopiable page 192.

Geo logs

These recording sheets (see the illustration above) could involve children in reflection over a longer period. A diary format would be appropriate for a personal record of their geographical learning over the year and would invite children to write or draw in response to specific aspects of their work. These could also become a more general learning log. Children could design their own logs and decorate them with small illustrations and borders with an appropriate geographical theme.

Reflections

Assessment and record-keeping must be supportive to both teachers and children. Evaluation is part of any teaching and learning process and must be undertaken on a regular and systematic basis using different strategies. Subjectivity, like bias, inevitably creeps into assessment procedures through personal relationships, preferences for different forms of activities, and interpretations of content and each other's expectations. Clearly, both are rooted in human experience, but their recognition makes it possible to minimise their impact upon evaluation.

Assessment requires that the children and the teachers work towards shared goals and that they both learn to talk, listen and observe effectively. Positive encouragement gains meaning through being specific. Constructive criticism works best where there is trust and openness.

Geography can play a very positive role in children's development. Its broadly-based concerns with self, society and setting (through the study of place, people and environmental processes) encourage and derive from children having an understanding about themselves and the world around them. This understanding involves appreciating the diversity of ideas, belief systems and patterns of behaviour. Finding ways to distil the world's complexity into a framework of understanding, requires learning to make balanced and independent judgements on the strength of accurate and informed interpretations.

Reflection and evaluation are integral to this search for meaning. Finding ways to develop effective assessment procedures which neither trivialise geographical experiences, nor underestimate the breadth of children's capacity for understanding, underpin planning a place for geography in the primary curriculum.

On a wider scale, developing children's ability to reflect upon their own work, actions and thinking has further significance. The study of geography involves children in learning about the influence of human activity and decisions upon the diverse cultural, physical and natural environments of the world. It informs and illuminates children's awareness of the state of the earth, its people and the diversity of all its life-forms. It helps children to appreciate that the need for social and environmental responsibility operates at every scale and involves everyone, including themselves.

Children have a right to a knowledge and understanding of processes and patterns which shape the changes and continuities in the world around them; they also have an entitlement to geography in the primary curriculum. This book urges teachers to consider geography as an important element in children's development. Its purpose has been to raise possibilities, encourage learning opportunities, and foster critical awareness through geographical understanding. It is simply a springboard from which teachers should be encouraged to explore other geographical possibilities. May this book help to foster a global consciousness attuned to the needs of our planet into the twenty-first century.

CHAPTER 15

Resources

Useful addresses

Action Aid,
Hamlyn House,
Archway,
London
N19 5PG

Amnesty International,
99 Rosebury Avenue,
London
EC1R 4RE

British Society of Soil Science
(BSSS),
Information and Publicity
Officer,
The Old Bakery,
25 Westbury Road,
Edington.
Nr Bath,
Avon
BA13 4QR

CAFOD,
2 Romero Close,
Stockwell Road,
London
SW9 9TY

Council for Environmental
Education,
University of Reading
London Road
Reading
RG1 5AQ

Christian Aid,
PO Box 100,
35-41 Lower Marsh,
London
SE1 7RL

The Civic Trust,
17 Carlton House Terrace,
London
SW1Y 5AW

Commission for Racial
Equality,
Elliott House,
10/12 Allington Street,
London
SW1E 5EH

Commission of the European
Communities (UK Office),
Jean Monnet House,
8 Storey's Gate,
London
SW1P 3AT

The Commonwealth Institute,
The Education Resource
Centre,
Kensington High Street,
London
W8 6NQ

Council for International
Understanding,
Meadowlea House,
86 Littleham Road,
Exmouth,
Devon
EX8 2QT

Countryside Commission,
John Dower House,
Crescent Place,
Cheltenham,
Gloucestershire
GL50 3RA

DFE (International Relations
Division),
Grove House,
2-6 Orange Street,
London
WC2H 7WE

The Documentation Centre for
Education in Europe,
BP 431 R6
F67006 Strasbourg,
Cedex,
France

The European Movement,
Europe House,
158 Buckingham Palace Road,
London
SW1 9TR

European Parliament (Europe),
Information & Public Relations,
Eastman Building,
89-92 Rue Belliard,
1040 Brussels,
Belgium

Eurotunnel Exhibition Centre,
St. Martin's Plain,
Cheriton High Street,
Folkestone,
Kent
CT19 4QD

Friends of the Earth,
26-28 Underwood Street,
London
N1 7QJ

Friends of the Earth (Europe
Office),
Rue Blanche 29,
1050 Brussels,
Belgium

The Geographical Association,
343 Fulwood Road,
Sheffield
S10 3BP

Information and
Documentation Centre for the
Geography of the Netherlands,
Heidelberglan 2,
Postbus 80115,
3508 TC Utrecht,
The Netherlands

League for the Exchange of
Commonwealth Teachers,
Commonwealth House,
7 Lion Yard,
Tremadoc Road,
Clapham,
London
SW4 7NF

Media Natura,
45 Shelton Street,
London
WC2H 9HJ

NADEC (National Association of
Development Education
Centres),
6 Endsleigh Street,
London
WC1H 0HX

NCET (National Council for
Education Technology),
Sir William Lyons Road,
University of Warwick Science
Park,
Coventry
CV4 7AL

Overseas Development
Administration (ODA),
The Foreign & Commonwealth
Office,
Information Department,
Room E918 Eland House,
Stag Place,
London
SW1E 5DH

Oxfam Primary Education Unit,
46A Stoke Newington Church
Street,
London
N16 0LU

Save the Children,
Education Unit,
Mary Datchelor House,

17 Grove Lane,
London
SE5 8RD

Survival International,
310 Edgeware Road,
London
W2 1DY

Trocaire,
The Catholic World
Development Agency,
169 Booterstown Avenue,
Blackrock,
Co. Dublin,
Republic of Ireland

UNICEF-UK,
55 Lincoln's Inn Fields,
London
WC2A 3NB

United Kingdom Centre for
European Education,
Seymour Mews House,
Seymour Mews,
London
W1H 9PE

Worldwide Fund for Nature
(WWF),
Panda House,
Wayside Park,
Godalming,
Surrey
GU7 1XR

Other helpful organisations

Development and multi-
cultural education centres;
national tourist offices;
consulates and higher
commissions; local Members
of the European Parliament;
VSO returned volunteers; LEAs;
teacher's centres; secondary
schools; FHE colleges;
Chambers of Commerce;
twinning associations; local
libraries and language
societies; planning
departments; museums loan
services and so on.

Reading around

Stories for geography

Armitage, R. & D. (1991) *The Lighthouse Keeper's Rescue* Andre Deutsch

Baker, J. (1988) *Where the Forest Meets the Sea* Walker

Cameron, A. (1992) *The Most Beautiful Place in the World* Doubleday

Cooke, T. (1989) *Mammy, sugar falling down* Beaver

Dahl, R. (1991) *Fantastic Mr Fox* Young Puffin

Daly, N. (1987) *Not so fast Songololo* Picture Puffin

Desai, A. (1989) *The Village by the Sea* Penguin

Flindall, J. (1990) *The Journey Home* Walker

Gray, N. (1991) *A Balloon for Grandad* Collins

Grifalconi, A. (1989) *The Village of Round and Square Houses* Macmillan

Hayes, R. (1989) *The Fox in the Wood* Anglia Young Books

Hedderwick, M. (1989) *Katie Morag and the tiresome teddy* Collins

Hicyilmac, G. (1991) *Against the Storm* Puffin

Hughes, S. (1988) *When we went to the park* Walker

Hutchins, P. (1978) *Don't Forget the Bacon* Bodley Head

Hutchins, P. (1992) *Rosie's Walk* Bodley Head

Jonas, A. (1992) *The Quilt* Walker

Keeping, C. (1989) *Adam and Paradise Island* OUP

Lawrence, A. (1988) *The Travels of Oggy* Chivers

Loverseed, A. (1990) *Tikkatoo's Journey* Blackie

Naidoo, B. (1987) *Journey to Jo'burg* Armada

Ungerer, T. (1977) *The Three Robbers* Methuen

Waddell, M. (1985) *Going West* Puffin

Wallace, K. (1992) *The Battle for Gold-diggers Forest* Simon & Schuster

Westall, R. (1992) *Stormsearch* Puffin

Recommended books

Bridges, C. & Scoffham, S. (1992) *Blueprints Geography* Stanley Thornes

Bowles, Rachel (1993) *Resources – primary geography* The Geography Association

Chambers, B. & Morgan, W. (1991) *Ginn Geography: Big Book* and *Teachers' Resource Book for Key Stage 1* Ginn & Co. Ltd.

Foley, M. & Janikoun (1992) *The Really Practical Guide to Primary Geography* Stanley Thornes

ODEC (1992) *Book for Keeps*, 2nd Edition Oxford Development Centre

Pike, G. & Seeley, D. (1989) *Global Teacher, Global Learner* Hodder & Stoughton

UNICEF (1991) *Songs, games & stories from around the World* UNICEF

Atlas

The Picture Atlas of the World (1992) Dorling Kindersley Ltd

Keystart UK Atlas & World Atlas Programme (1992) Collins-Longman

Philip's Wildlife Atlas (1992) George Philip Ltd

Philip's Environmental Atlas (1992) George Philip Ltd

The Reader's Digest World Atlas (1991) Reader's Digest

A T CHART

The text on this page refers to the National Curriculum for England and Wales. Use the chart to identify the attainment targets covered by the activities in this book. Activities are identified by their chapter number which is in bold, and then the activity number; for example **7**/2 means Chapter 7, Activity 2.

AT \ Level	1 *Geographical skills*	2 *Knowledge and understanding of places*	3 *Physical geography*	4 *Human geography*	5 *Environmental geography*
1	**1**/1,2,3,4,5,6,7; **2**/1,2,3,4,5,6,7,8; **3**/1,2,3,4,5,6,7,8, 9,10,11; **4**/1,2,5,7; **5**/1,4,7; **6**/1,2,3,4, 5,6,7,8; **7**/1,2,3,4, 5,6,7,8,9; **8**/2,3; **9**/1,2,3,4,5,6,7,8, 9,11; **10**/1,2,3,4, 5,6	**1**/2,4,5,6,7; **2**/1,2,3,4,5,6,7; **3**/2,3,7,8,10,11; **4**/1,2,3,4,5,6,7; **5**/1,2,3,4,5,6; **6**/1,2,3,4,5,6,7,8; **7**/1,2,3,4,6,7,8,9 **8**/2,3; **9**/1,3,4,5, 6,7,8,9,10,ll; **10**/1,2,3,4,5,6	**2**/2,4,5,7; **5**/1,2,4,5,6; **7**/8; **10**/4,5	**1**/3,4,5,6,7; **2**/1,2,3,4,5,6; **3**/9; **4**/1,4,5; **5**/1; **6**/1,2,3,4, 5,6,7,8; **7**/3,4, 6,7,8,9,10; **8**/1,2,3; **9**/1,2, 3,4,7,9,10; **10**/1,2,4,5,6	**1**/3,4,5; **2**/2,3,4,5,6,7,8; **3**/8; **4**/2,4,5,6; **5**/1,4,5; **6**/3,6,7, 8; **7**/1,2,5,9,10; **9**/8; **10**/5
2	**1**/1,2,4,5,6,7; **2**/1,2,3,4,5,6,7,8; **3**/1,2,3,4,5,6,7,8, 9,10,11; **4**/1,2,3, 4,5,6,7; **5**/1,2,4, 5,6,7; **6**/1,2,3,4, 5,6,7,8; **7**/1,2,3, 4,5,6,7,8,9; **8**/1,2,3; **9**/1,2,3, 4,5,6,7,8,9,10,11; **10**/1,2,3,4,5,6	**1**/1,3,6,7; **2**/1,2,3, 4,5,6,7; **3**/2,5,7,8, 10,11; **4**/1,2,3,4,5, 6,7; **5**/1,2,3,4,5,6, 7,8; **6**/1,2,3,4,5,6, 7; **7**/1,2,3,4,5,6,7, 8,9,10; **8**/2,3; **9**/1,3,4,5,7,8,9,10, 11; **10**/1,2,3,4,5,6	**2**/2,4,5,6,7; **5**/1,2,5,7; **7**/2,8; **10**/4	**1**/2,3,4,5,6,7; **2**/1,2,3,4,5,6; **3**/9; **4**/1,4,5; **5**/1,3,4,5; **6**/1,2,3,4,5,6,8; **7**/4,6,7,8,9,10; **8**/1,2,3; **9**/1,3, 4,5,7,9; **10**/1,2, 4,6	**1**/2,4,5; **2**/2,3,4,5,6,7,8; **3**/8; **4**/4,5; **5**/1,2,4,5; **6**/3,6,7,8; **7**/2,4,5,6,7,8,9, 10; **9**/10; **10**/3
3	**1**/1,3,5,6,7; **2**/1,2, 3,4,5,6,7,8; **3**/1,2, 3,4,5,6,8,9,10,ll; **4**/1,4; **5**/4,7; **6**/1,3,4,6,7,8; **7**/3, 4,5,6,7,8; **8**/1,2; **9**/10,11; **10**/3	**2**/1,3,4,5,6; **3**/1,2,5,8; **4**/3,4; **5**/2,4,5,6; **6**/2,4,6,7,8; **7**/3,6,7,10; **9**/1,3,4,5,7,10	**1**/1; **2**/3,4,5, 6,7; **3**/3; **4**/1,2,3,5; **5**/1,2,4,5,6,7; **9**/1,3,4,6,7,8, 10; **10**/4	**1**/1; **2**/1,2,3,4, 5,6; **3**/9; **4**/1; **5**/1,2,4; **6**/2,3,6,7,8; **7**/3,6,7,9,10; **8**/2; **9**/1,4,5, 7,10; **10**/4,5,6	**1**/4,5; **2**/2,3,4, 5,6,7,8; **3**/8; **4**/4,5; **5**/1,5; **6**/3,6,7,8; **7**/2,4,5,6,7, 8,10; **10**/3
4	**2**/1,3,5; **3**/4,5,6,7, 8; **4**/1,7; **5**/7; **6**/2, 8; **7**/5; **9**/7,1; **10**/6	**2**/4,5; **5**/2,3; **7**/6,7; **9**/7	**2**/1,7; **4**/3; **5**/1,2,3,6,7; **10**/4	**3**/9; **5**/7; **6**/8; **9**/7	**2**/3,4,5; **4**/3; **5**/2; **6**/3
5	**3**/4				

Note: Many activities in this book could be extended to cover Levels 4 and 5 but as many pupils will be working at Levels 1 to 3, references have focused on these levels.

PHOTOCOPIABLES

The pages in this section can be photocopied and adapted to suit your own needs and those of your class; they do not need to be declared in respect of any photocopying licence. Eight general photocopiable pages, including five blank outline maps, a blank grid and two self-assessment sheets, are provided along with five other pages which relate to specific activities within the main body of the book. Appropriate page and activity references are given at the top of each page for quick reference.

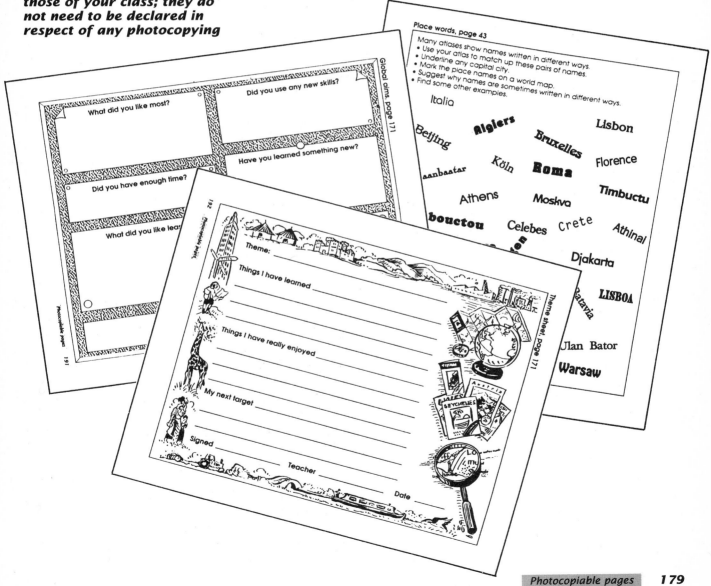

Global aims, page 171

What did you like most?

Did you use any new skills?

Have you learned something new?

Did you have enough time?

What did you like least?

Photocopiable pages

191

192

Photocopiable pages

Theme sheet, page 171

Theme: _____

Things I have learned _____

Things I have really enjoyed _____

My next target _____

Signed _____

Teacher _____ Date _____

Place words, page 43

Many atlases show names written in different ways.
• Use your atlas to match up these pairs of names.
• Underline any capital city.
• Mark the place names on a world map.
• Suggest why names are sometimes written in different ways.
• Find some other examples.

Italia

Beijing   Algiers   Bruxelles   Lisbon

...anbaatar   Köln   Roma   Florence

Athens   Moskva   Timbuctu

...bouctou   Celebes   Crete   Athinai

Djakarta

LISBOA

...atavia

Ulan Bator

Warsaw

The British Isles

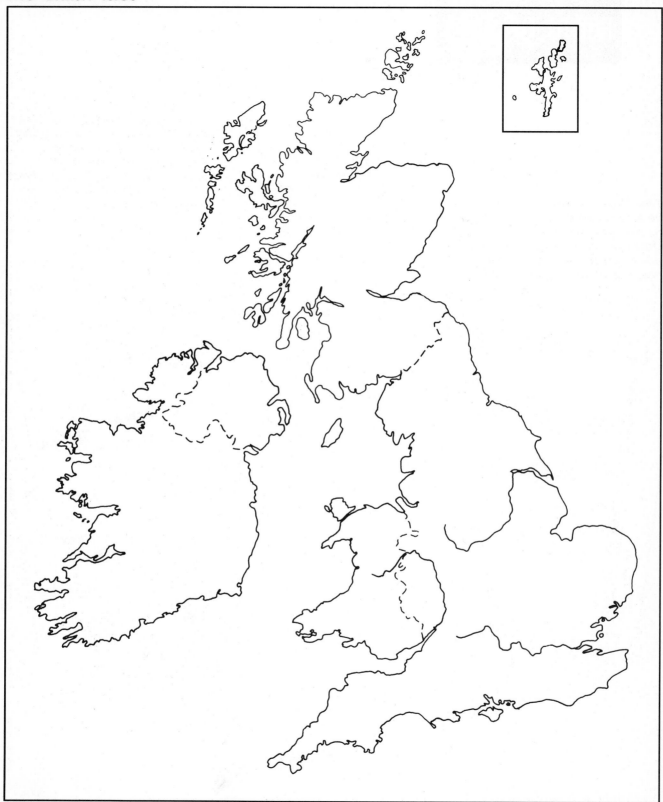

Europe

The World – 1

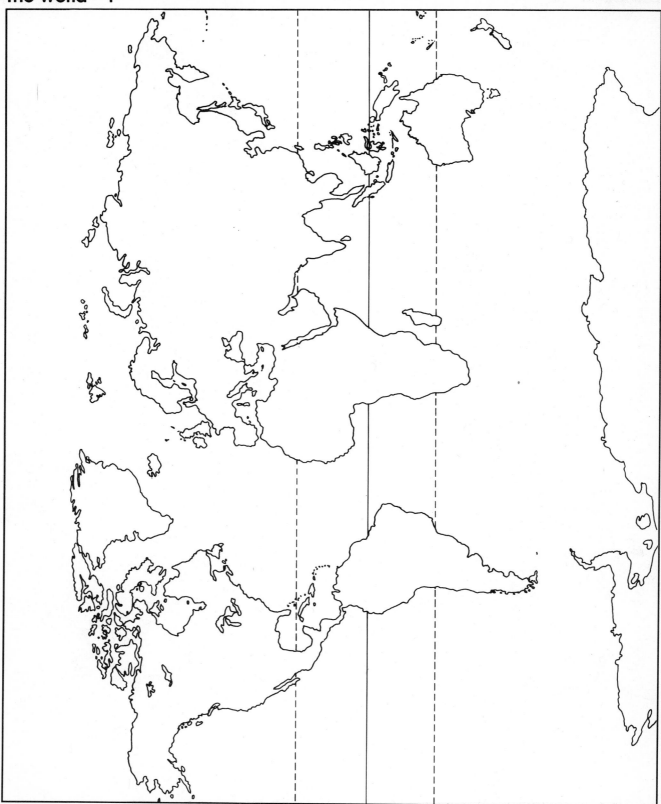

The World – 2

Cosy corners, page 14

Name: _____ **Date:** _____ **Time:** _____

Study area: _____ **Season:** _____

Ring the words which best describe each site you visit in your study area.

Site A
windy/sheltered old/new
warm/cool clean/dirty
sunny/shaded boring/interesting
busy/peaceful bright/dull
noisy/quiet attractive/unattractive

Site B
windy/sheltered old/new
warm/cool clean/dirty
sunny/shaded boring/interesting
busy/peaceful bright/dull
noisy/quiet attractive/unattractive

Site C
windy/sheltered old/new
warm/cool clean/dirty
sunny/shaded boring/interesting
busy/peaceful bright/dull
noisy/quiet attractive/unattractive

Site D
windy/sheltered old/new
warm/cool clean/dirty
sunny/shaded boring/interesting
busy/peaceful bright/dull
noisy/quiet attractive/unattractive

Add some of your own words to describe each site.

Answer these questions at each site:
1. What do you like most?
2. What do you like least?
3. How might this site be improved?

Site A
1.
2.
3.

Site B
1.
2.
3.

Site C
1.
2.
3.

Site D
1.
2.
3.

Postal survey, page 16

Name(s): _____ Length of survey: _____

Survey point: _____ from: _____ to: _____

Total number of letters sent (S) received (R)	Posted locally		Posted within the county		Posted within the country		Posted within Europe		Posted outside Europe		Other postal deliveries - parcels etc
	(S)	(R)	(S)	(R)	(S)	(R)	(S)	(R)	(S)	(R)	
Sample:											

Add any other interesting information about your postal survey here:
e.g. average journey time of received letters
shortest journey time
longest distance
mode of transport

Finding where you are, page 39

	A	B	C	D
5				
4				
3				
2				
1				

Many atlases show names written in different ways.
- Use your atlas to match up these pairs of names.
- Underline any capital city.
- Mark the place names on a world map.
- Suggest why names are sometimes written in different ways.
- Find some other examples.

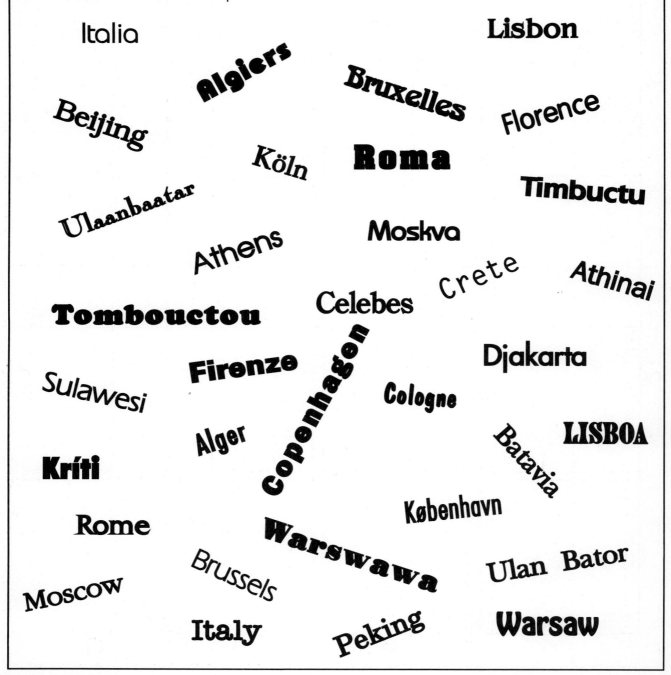

Italia

Lisbon

Algiers

Bruxelles

Beijing

Florence

Köln

Roma

Ulaanbaatar

Timbuctu

Athens

Moskva

Crete

Athinai

Tombouctou

Celebes

Djakarta

Firenze

Copenhagen

Cologne

Sulawesi

LISBOA

Alger

Batavia

Kríti

Rome

København

Warswawa

Ulan Bator

Moscow

Brussels

Italy

Peking

Warsaw

Mappable allsorts, page 44

Type of map or plan	What does it show?	Where might it be used?	Who might use it?
Town map			
Underground map			
Shopping centre plan			
Tourist map of national park			
Air route map of world			

Name _____ Date_____

Title _____

Names of characters: _____

_____

Where does the journey start? _____

_____

What is the reason for the journey? _____

_____

How do the characters travel? _____

_____

Things/places passed on the way: _____

_____

How long does the journey take? _____

_____

Where does the journey end? _____

_____

How far did the characters travel? _____

_____

Did you use any new skills?

Have you learned something new?

What might you do differently next time?

Did you work well with others?

What did you like most?

Did you have enough time?

What did you like least?

Theme: _____

Things I have learned _____

Things I have really enjoyed _____

My next target _____

Signed _____ **Teacher** _____ **Date** _____